THE GREAT ENCOUNTER
OF CHINA AND THE WEST,
1500–1800

CRITICAL ISSUES IN HISTORY

World and International History

American History

THE GREAT ENCOUNTER OF CHINA AND THE WEST, 1500–1800

THIRD EDITION

D. E. MUNGELLO

ROWMAN & LITTLEFIELD PUBLISHERS, INC.
Lanham • Boulder • New York • Toronto • Plymouth, UK

ROWMAN & LITTLEFIELD PUBLISHERS, INC.

Published in the United States of America
by Rowman & Littlefield Publishers, Inc.
A wholly owned subsidiary of The Rowman & Littlefield Publishing Group, Inc.
4501 Forbes Boulevard, Suite 200, Lanham, Maryland 20706
www.rowmanlittlefield.com

Estover Road, Plymouth PL6 7PY, United Kingdom

British Library Cataloging in Publication Information Available

Library of Congress Cataloging-in-Publication Data
Mungello, David E., 1943-
   The great encounter of China and the West, 1500-1800 / D.E. Mungello. —
3rd ed.
      p. cm. — (Critical issues in history)
   Includes bibliographical references and index.
   ISBN-13: 978-0-7425-5797-0 (cloth : alk. paper)
   ISBN-10: 0-7425-5797-9 (cloth : alk. paper)
   ISBN-13: 978-0-7425-5798-7 (pbk. : alk. paper)
   ISBN-10: 0-7425-5798-7 (pbk. : alk. paper)
   [etc.]
   1. China—Civilization—Western influences. 2. Europe—Civilization—
Chinese influences. 3. East and West. 4. China—History—Ming Dynasty,
1368–1644. 5. China—History—Qing Dynasty, 1644-1912. I. Title.
DS750.72.M86 2009
303.48'251040903—dc22

                                                                    2008052774

Printed in the United States of America

♾™ The paper used in this publication meets the minimum requirements of
American National Standard for Information Sciences—Permanence of Paper for
Printed Library Materials, ANSI/NISO Z39.48-1992.

CONTENTS

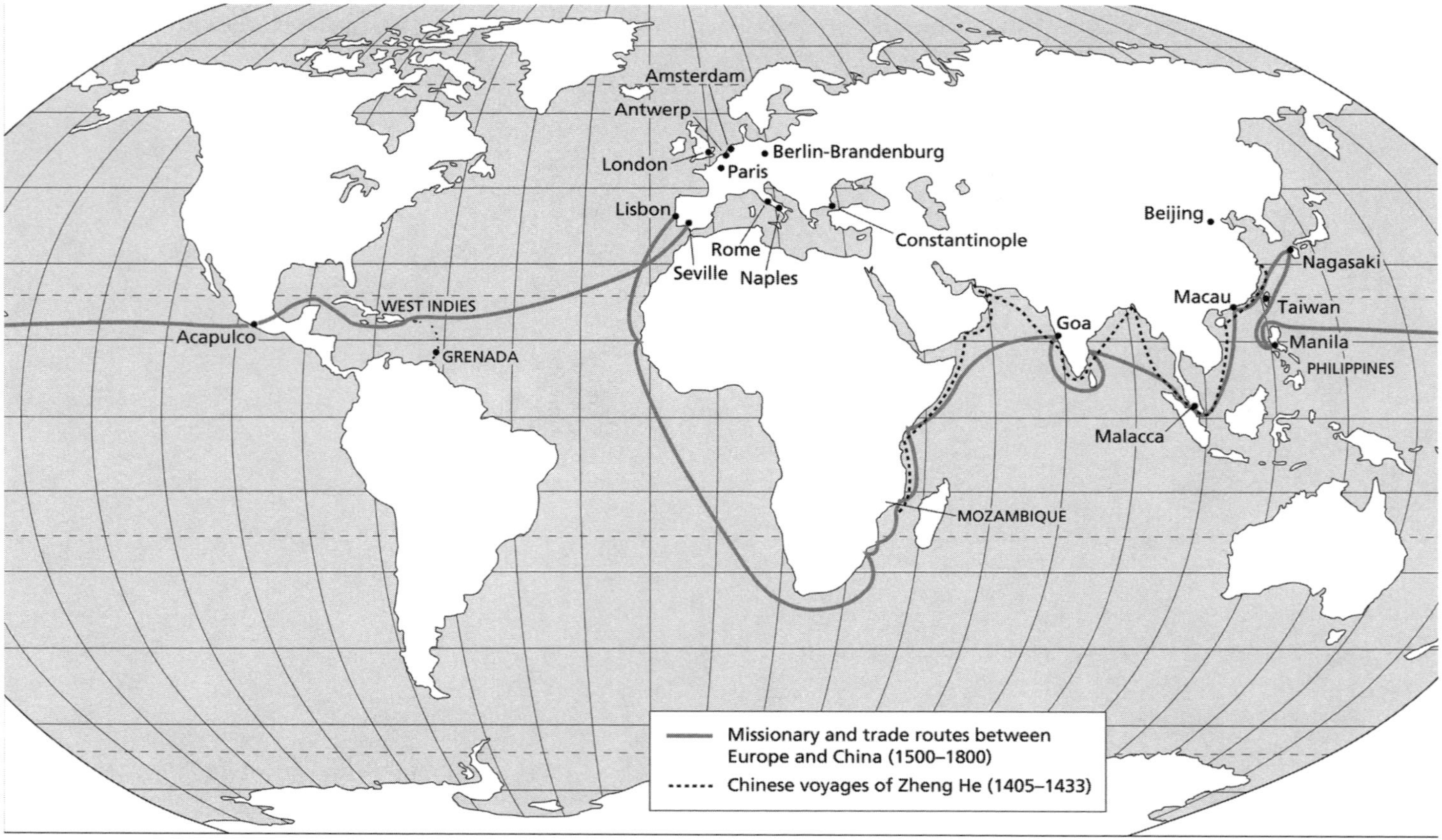
Amsterdam
Antwerp
London
Paris
Berlin-Brandenburg
Lisbon
Rome
Seville
Naples
Constantinople
Beijing
Nagasaki
Macau
Taiwan
Manila
PHILIPPINES
Goa
Malacca
MOZAMBIQUE
WEST INDIES
GRENADA
Acapulco
Missionary and trade routes between Europe and China (1500–1800)
Chinese voyages of Zheng He (1405–1433)

Map 1

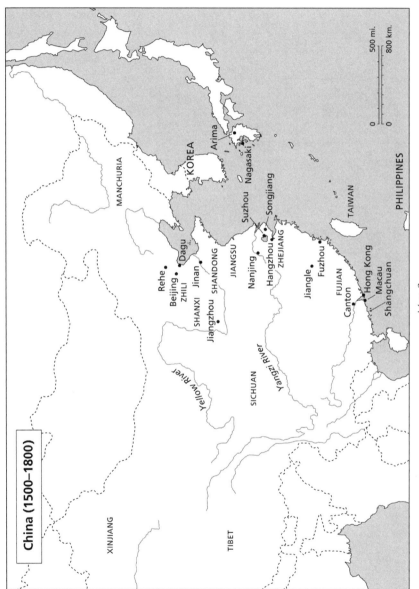

China (1500–1800)

Map 2

ILLUSTRATIONS

PREFACE

The growing importance of China in today's world has stimulated a great deal of new research on the historical relationship of China and the West. The third edition of this book attempts to incorporate this new research into the second edition's narrative of Sino-Western history, particularly in the areas of biographies, sexuality, gender, and the history of sensibilities.

This book is written for the history student and general reader. Because the aim is to present information and ideas in the most clear and meaningful manner, the scholarly apparatus has been reduced to a minimum. Technical terms are explained in the text. While the technicalities have been reduced to a minimum, the ideas in this book are intended to be substantive and challenging. Although footnotes have been omitted, the sources I consulted are listed at the end of each chapter. Because of the less specialized nature of the readership, most foreign-language sources have been omitted. Chinese sources are mentioned in the text rather than in the chapter bibliographies. For those readers interested in fuller bibliographical treatment, I would refer them to my other works that cover many of the same subjects in greater detail.

The ten intervening years since publication of the first edition have served to confirm the historical patterns of 1500–1800 and 1800–1997 that were defined in the first edition. Nevertheless some fine-tuning of the second cycle has been appropriate. No colony was more significant to the Sino-Western encounter of 1500–1800 than Macau. With its transfer from Portugal to China on 20 December 1999 (two and a half years after the transfer of British Hong Kong to China), it becomes appropriate to round off the date of the cycle 1800–1997 to 1800–2000.

One deficiency of the first edition was its lack of stories with a human dimension. In an attempt to better balance the intellectual, religious, and artistic emphases of the first edition, I have added narratives dealing with the joys, struggles, victories, and tragedies of people who participated in these major cycles of history. In particular, I have added material dealing with women, female infanticide, male homosexuality, music, and technology, which I hope will allow the book to come alive to readers in ways that the first edition did not. One-quarter of the illustrations in the third edition are new. I have also tried to correct a second deficiency of the first edition in its overly simplistic treatment of Sinocentrism (Chinese ethnic superiority). A growing body of recent research has shown that Sinocentrism was an idealized view of China's place in the world that did not always reflect the reality of Chinese history.

The most common way of referring to a Chinese emperor since the Ming dynasty (1368–1644) is by his reign-title (*nienhao*) rather than by his given name. The term "Kangxi" is a reign-title rather than a name, and this explains why this book refers to the "Kangxi Emperor" rather than to "Emperor Kangxi." For similar reasons, we would refer to President Franklin Delano Roosevelt as the "New Deal President" rather than "President New Deal." Of course, the Kangxi Emperor had a name, several in fact. He was formally named Xuanye, and he is sometimes called by his posthumous temple-name, Emperor Shengzu, but this is a complication that is best avoided in such a short work. The same situation applies to other emperors mentioned in this book, such as the Chongzhen Emperor, the Shunzhi Emperor, and the Qianlong Emperor. The pinyin system of romanization of Chinese characters has been used.

The illustrations are an integral and important part of this book, and I am indebted to several people who assisted in locating, interpreting, and securing the use of these illustrations. These include Professor Michele Fatica of the Università degli Studi di Napoli "l'Orientale" (Naples), Dr. Theodore N. Foss of the Center for East Asian Studies of the University of Chicago, Professor Harold Kahn of Stanford University, Professor Takata Tokio of the Institute for Research in Humanities at Kyoto, and Dr. R. G. Tiedemann of the Centre for the Study of Christianity in China, King's College London. Dr. Adrian Dudink of the Catholic University of Leuven assisted with the illustration "The Four Last Things" (*Wanmin simo tu*). Dr. Maxwell K. Hearn of the Department of Asian Art of the Metropolitan Museum of Art in New York assisted with the image from the Qianlong Emperor's Southern Inspection Tour.

Good books cannot be produced without good editors, and I would like to express a special note of thanks to the editorial director Ms. Susan McEachern and to the production editor Ms. Alden Perkins. Finally, I would like to express my gratitude to Baylor University and to the Department of History for their support of this project.

Once more, I dedicate this book to the memory of my late wife. Christine McKegg Mungello (1946–1997), *requiescat in pace*.

1

HISTORICAL OVERVIEW

CHINA'S RETURN TO GREATNESS

For two weeks in August of 2008, the attention of the world was focused on the Beijing Olympics. For the Chinese, this was far more than a sports event. It was an attempt to restore China's past greatness and remove the lingering memories of history's humiliations. To achieve that goal, the Chinese surpassed all previous Olympic nation-sponsors by spending $42 billion for the Beijing games. These funds were used to build the Bird's Nest stadium, which seated ninety-one thousand people; an aquatics center; a new airport terminal; and new roads, subways, and more. China's extravagance caused other Olympic efforts to pale by comparison. The $15 billion spent at the 2004 Athens Olympics drove Greece into debt while the British are already bickering over the costs of the 2012 London Olympics. However, the goal was so important to the Chinese that their government felt justified in spending this vast sum. The expenditure also had political benefits. Public enthusiasm for the Olympics diverted the economic discontent of the millions of poor who had been left out of China's prosperity. In addition, it drowned out political demands from the Tibetans and Muslim Uighurs for greater autonomy, and it overshadowed China's flawed human rights record. China's investment was amply rewarded. Although the United States achieved the greatest total of medals (gold, silver, and bronze), China received the greatest number of gold medals. This confirmed China's newfound status as the chief world challenger to the United States.

If we use the longer perspective provided by history, we see that the notion of China as a world power is not new, but rather a return to the past. Chinese nationalism involves more than a nation-state. It is a form of ethnocentrism with ancient roots. The Olympics triumph eased the lingering

1

memories of humiliation inflicted on China by Western imperialist nations in the nineteenth and twentieth centuries. During that time, China declined into an outmoded empire that failed to come to terms with the modern world until it was practically swallowed by the imperialist powers. Even the founder of communism, Karl Marx, wrote in the *New York Daily Tribune* in 1858 that China was "a giant empire . . . vegetating in the teeth of time, insulated by the forced exclusion of general intercourse, and thus continuing to dupe itself with delusion of Celestial perfection."

The dominant Western view of China during the past fifty years has been a heritage of the American victory in World War II (1941–1945). Historians used the polarity of tradition (as exemplified by a downtrodden China) and modernity (as exemplified by a triumphant United States) to explain recent Chinese history. Drawing from nineteenth-century images of China as a static and unchanging society, many historians said that China was unable to generate significant change internally and could only be transformed from the outside by the impact of the West. This was called the "impact and response" thesis. It was widely propagated in the influential textbook of East Asian history by the Harvard historians John K. Fairbank and Edwin O. Reischauer who subtitled the two volumes of their work *The Great Tradition* (1958) and *The Modern Transformation* (1960).

My mentor at Berkeley and one of Fairbank's students, Joseph R. Levenson, gave the most eloquent explanation of the end of Chinese tradition in his trilogy *Confucian China and Its Modern Fate* (1958–1965). For Levenson, Chinese tradition existed only as a fascinating antique, hopelessly outdated in the modern world. His book was widely praised as brilliant, but brilliant books can be wrong, and Levenson's thesis has been abandoned with the passage of time. Criticism of the view of traditional China as a static culture began in the 1970s when American confidence was shaken by a frustrating war in Vietnam (1964–1973). Led by the Columbia scholar Wm. Theodore de Bary, China scholars began to interpret traditional Chinese culture in a more favorable light. Instead of viewing the Confucian tradition as stagnant, de Bary viewed it as a dynamic force that continued into the present day.

This book is based upon looking back into the past before China's decline. During the period 1500–1800 China was widely viewed as a dynamic culture, a world power, and the greatest nation in the world. Europe, by contrast, was merely in the process of emerging, while the United States was still a beautiful wilderness. In fact, Europe had just reached its low point.

In 1453 the Byzantine capital of Constantinople finally fell to the Ottoman Turks, and a great historical, religious, political, and commercial bastion was detached from the rest of European civilization. Eastern and central Europe would now be threatened by the Muslim Turks for the next two centuries. In many respects, this was the nadir of European civilization in early modern history. At this point, the greatness of Hellenistic Greece and Rome were mere memories from the past, and Europe's future ascent was not yet visible. By contrast, in 1453 no nation in the world shined brighter than China. By standard criteria such as size, population, agriculture, commerce, wealth, sophistication, technology, military might, cuisine, learning, literature, and the fine arts, the Ming dynasty presided over the greatest nation in the world. China's 160 million people represented one-fourth of the total world population of six to seven hundred million in 1700.

SINOCENTRISM

The Chinese had the ability to mount distant naval voyages and had done so in the years 1405–1433 when enormous Chinese fleets traveled throughout the Indian Ocean as far as southern Arabia, east Africa, and Mozambique (see map 1). However, after these voyages ended, China's cultural and political preeminence, wealth, and concern with external threats to its security led the Chinese to turn inward, initially on the governmental level and later in the cultural sphere. When the Portuguese explorer Vasco da Gama sailed around southern Africa and on to India in 1498, there were few signs left to indicate to Europeans that the Chinese had made voyages in this region earlier in that century.

The Ming dynasty (1368–1644) had been established by some remarkably capable rulers who had organized a system of government that would last, largely unchanged, for over five hundred years. The foundations of the Ming were so well laid that the positive effects of good government and prosperity would continue for two centuries, or well into the sixteenth century. Agriculture thrived under the attention of a government that repaired and expanded canals and irrigation works and stocked public granaries. New strains of rice imported from Southeast Asia and new crops (maize, peanuts, and potatoes) imported from the Americas by way of the Philippines increased the food supply. The result was a healthier and more abundant population. Although commerce was disparaged by Confucian morality, it flourished. The Chinese export of silk, tea, and porcelains—the envy of the world—produced such a flow of silver from Spanish mines in Mexico and Peru that it, along with copper, displaced paper money. The Chinese use of silver as its prime form of currency absorbed as much as one-half of all the silver mined in South America in the early 1600s. Chinese manufactured goods like textiles were so much better than Spanish or Mexican textiles that they dominated the Mexican markets.

The Chinese view of the rest of the world in 1500 was a result of approximately thirty-five hundred years of historical development in which Chinese culture was the dominant influence in East Asia. Nations like Japan, Korea, and Vietnam had all been fundamentally shaped by the Chinese written language, by the Chinese imperial system, and by Confucian teachings that emphasized, on one hand, a hierarchical familial, political, and social order and, on the other hand, the selection of government officials on the egalitarian principle of literary examinations.

During China's early history, geographical separation from the rest of the world fostered a Chinese ethnocentrism, or Sinocentrism. (The root "Sino" [Chinese] and terms such as "Sinology" [the study of China] are derived from the Latin term for "Chinese," *Sinae*.) Chinese regarded their country as the center of the world and named it the "Middle Kingdom" (*Zhongguo*), in contrast to the "foreign kingdoms" (*waiguo*) in the rest of the world. The emperor of China, referred to as the "Son of Heaven" (*Tianzi*), was believed to rule with the mandate and authority of Heaven. According to traditional Chinese cosmology, the organization of mankind on the earth should duplicate the pattern found in the heavens. In this way of thinking, the Chinese emperor was compared to the polestar. Just as the other stars revolved around it, so too did other humans revolve in hierarchical order around the emperor. China's view of the rest of the world was an extension of this highly idealized system in terms of seeing other countries in a hierarchical and nonegalitarian manner.

For China, the non-Chinese world consisted of three zones. The first included a Sinitic zone of countries that were the closest geographically and that had borrowed extensively from Chinese culture. These included Korea, Vietnam, the Liuqiu (Ryukyu) Islands, and sometimes Japan. The second was an Inner Asian zone that consisted of people who were both ethnically and culturally non-Chinese. Whereas the Sinitic zone bordered on the east and south of China, the Inner Asian zone bordered on the north and west and included Manchuria, Mongolia, the Uighur territory, and Tibet. The third division was an outer zone that consisted of "outer barbarians" (*waiyi*) and included Southeast Asia, South Asia, and Europe.

The theory and the reality did not always match in Chinese history. In the traditional theory, the Chinese viewed all non-Chinese states as inferior and expected them to be tributary states. The Chinese emperor was supposed to rule by virtue of his superior human qualities. The favor that he bestowed was to be dispensed not only to Chinese but also to barbarians. To receive this imperial favor, the barbarians were to travel to the imperial court "to be transformed" (*laihua*). Over the centuries, these foreign lands sent embassies to the Chinese capital carrying gifts in the form of tribute signifying their subservient status to the Chinese. In turn, they received the rewards of the emperor's benevolent paternalism, which sometimes represented an amount that had been previously negotiated to appease a foreign military threat to the Chinese. The court reception of these foreign embassies involved an elaborate guest ritual that required foreigners to perform the kowtow (*koutou*), a triple genuflection and touching of the head to the ground nine times. Oftentimes these embassies included merchants, who were allowed to trade within clearly defined limits.

Sinocentrism ebbed and flowed with China's might and glory and was more prominent in some periods than in others. In the four centuries between the fall of the Han dynasty in AD 220 and the rise of the next great dynasty, the Tang, in 618, China was divided and became more receptive to foreign influences. During this time, the Chinese had substantial contact with Central and South Asians and were deeply influenced by them. Buddhism entered China and was assimilated into Chinese culture. The Tang dynasty (618–907) was one of the most cosmopolitan periods in Chinese history, and the influence of Buddhism peaked. Not only was there contact with India, Persia, and even Byzantium via the old Silk Route through Central Asia, but also numerous Arab traders from the Red Sea area established communities in southern Chinese ports. There was also extensive contact with Japan. Tang ceramic figurines portray a variety of racial types. The Song (960–1279) and Ming dynasties that followed were more Sinocentric with the reemergence of native Chinese traditions, particularly Confucianism.

The Qing dynasty (1644–1911) was the most successful of Chinese dynasties in terms of territorial expansion, all of which occurred prior to 1800. However, the Qing does not fit the model of Sinocentrism in which the Han culture assimilated (Sinified) non-Han peoples in China. The Manchus were a Tungusic tribal people who emerged to the northeast of China in present-day Manchuria. Their conquest of the Chinese was long lasting because of the hybrid origins of the empire they created. New research has shown that the Han Chinese literati did not dominate the Qing in ways previously believed. Rather, the Manchu conquerors imposed upon the Han Chinese literati bureaucracy an elite of imperial kinsmen and banner nobles. The Qing was a multiethnic state, and these disparate ethnic origins continue to generate Tibetan, Inner Mongolian, Uighur, and Taiwanese independence movements in our own time.

FOREIGN TRADE

Attitudes toward foreign trade can tell us a great deal about a nation. While poverty led European monarchs in the period 1500–1800 to promote foreign trade, China's wealth allowed Chinese monarchs to restrict it. Chinese emperors limited foreign trade on the grounds that it threatened national security. Although Chinese merchants were eager to send ships to foreign lands in pursuit of wealth, they were impeded by governmental restrictions.

Throughout the fourteenth century, a series of trade limitations was imposed; for example, in 1394, ordinary Chinese were prohibited from using foreign perfumes and other foreign goods. Foreign trade was limited to those lands that stood in a tributary relationship to China. The pressure to trade became so great in the sixteenth century and the government's efforts to combat smuggling so fruitless that the ban on trading was partially lifted in 1567. The government attempted to control trade through a system of licensing private traders. All unlicensed traders who ventured abroad did so under threat of severe penalties, including beheading. Confucianism contained a strong philosophical bias against merchants, on the grounds that they were motivated by profit rather than human benevolence. Traditionally, merchants were ranked last (after literati, peasants, and craftsmen) among the four main classes. And yet the potential wealth to be obtained through commerce was so great that many people became merchants in spite of the obstacles and because of practical realities. Many literati who served as scholar-officials closed their eyes to numerous violations of the prohibitions on trade.

By the end of the Ming dynasty, the bans on coastal and foreign trade had been reimposed, and the Chinese who engaged in foreign trade were practically indistinguishable from pirates. The first Chinese to settle in Taiwan were a blend of pirates and merchants of contraband. In 1620–1660 a severe depression in the worldwide trading system disrupted the flow of silver into China, mainly from the Americas, and appears to have worsened inflation in the late Ming. The deterioration of the quality of Ming emperors and their inability to respond to problems hastened social disintegration. These conditions made it possible for the Manchus to move their armies into China. When the Manchus conquered the Ming capital of Beijing and established the Qing dynasty in 1644, the traders and pirates on the southeast coast allied themselves with the Ming loyalists. They were led in their fight against the Manchus by the swashbuckling pirate Zheng Chenggong (1624–1662), known in European accounts as Koxinga. Born to a Chinese father and a Japanese mother, Zheng was one of the first of a category of Chinese who lived abroad called "Overseas Chinese."

The exalted Manchu fighting prowess did not extend to sea warfare, and after suffering a series of humiliating naval defeats, the Manchus shifted tactics in 1660 and began evacuating the population from Chinese coastal areas ten miles inland to deprive these traders and pirates of their food and other supplies. The government burned the coastal towns and destroyed the local inhabitants' boats. This policy had the effect of eliminating China's maritime trade and created a vacuum that European nations, such as Portugal, Spain, and the Netherlands, filled. After Taiwan was conquered by the Manchus in 1683, foreign trade was allowed, but emigration was ruled out on the grounds that Overseas Chinese colonies would become bases of sedition against the government. Granting trade to foreigners was viewed as a way of controlling and manipulating them.

The last form of isolationism that the Chinese government was able to impose was the Canton System. In 1787 Canton was declared the sole legal port for foreign trade. This trade was conducted through a guild of merchants known as the Cohong. The Cohong was first established in 1760 with nine traders, later abolished, and rechartered in 1782 with twelve or thirteen merchants. Direct contact between the foreign traders and the Chinese government was forbidden, and all communications with the government had to be funneled through the Hoppo. This Cohong system lasted until the Opium War and the Treaty of Nanjing (1842) when the Chinese suffered the first in a series of disastrous defeats and unequal treaties, but this carries us beyond our concluding date of 1800.

European involvement in foreign trade was quite different. In the early 1500s, Europeans aspired to greatness but, unlike the Chinese, had not yet attained it. In 1494, Spain and Portugal had agreed to a proposal initiated by Pope Alexander VI and ratified in the Treaty of Tordesillas that divided the world evenly between these two countries, with a boundary line running down the middle of the North Atlantic Ocean and bisecting South America. Everything to the east of the line, including the Portuguese colony of Brazil, would fall within Portugal's jurisdiction, and everything to the west of that line, extending across the Pacific to the Philippines, would belong to Spain. This allowed the Portuguese to control the trade routes eastward to Asia and Africa while the Spanish controlled the westward trade routes to the Americas and onward to the Pacific Ocean and the Philippines (see map 1).

Portugal's official secrecy clouded accounts of its first contacts with China. The first recorded Portuguese visit to China was in 1514, and the first official Portuguese embassy was led by Tomé Pires from Malacca to Canton in 1517. The Chinese authorities in Canton permitted Pires to proceed to the capital, Beijing, where the envoy waited in vain from July 1520 to February 1521 for an audience with the emperor. Meanwhile the mis-behavior of Portuguese traders and sailors in south China—along with ac-cusations that the Portuguese were unscrupulous traders—poisoned the at-mosphere. Pires never did meet with the emperor, and when the Zhengde Emperor died in May of 1521, Pires and his entourage were ordered back to Canton, where they were imprisoned and their gifts for the emperor confiscated. The envoy and his staff died in prison, but not before sending out letters in 1524 that urged the Portuguese king to mount a military ex-pedition against China. Fortunately this campaign was never initiated, for it would have amounted to a mouse attacking a lion. (At this time, the popu-lation of Portugal was approximately 1 million and that of China 150 mil-lion.) Instead, the Portuguese more reasonably persisted in their efforts to trade through south China ports and circa 1555 established a trading settle-ment at Macau. The Portuguese colony of Macau survived for nearly 450 years and was absorbed by China in 1999.

Prior to 1800, the divisions among Europeans in contact with China were caused more by nationalistic and economic differences than by reli-gion. Almost all of the missionaries who went to China prior to 1800 were Catholic. Disputes between them were engendered by the dominant form of economic thinking at that time, mercantilism. Sometimes called "cash-box thinking," mercantilism viewed the accumulation of gold and silver in the national treasury to be the chief aim of economic policy. Because trad-ing partners were viewed in adversarial rather than cooperative terms, there was an emphasis on building large mercenary armies and navies to support the warlike competition for trade. Since economic interests were identified with national interests, a good deal of nationalistic rivalry arose. This rivalry spilled over to the missionaries who, although all Catholic, divided on na-tionalistic lines in mission policy.

MUTUAL INFLUENCE BETWEEN CHINA AND THE WEST

For three centuries, between 1500 and 1800, Europe and China had exten-sive contact, which exerted enormous influence. In this book, the term "West" is used synonymously with "Europe" not simply because this usage has become customary but also because the Chinese themselves during the period 1500–1800 commonly referred to Europe as the "Far West" (*Yuan Xi* or *Tai Xi*) and "Western Land" (*Xi du*). They also referred to Europe as the "Western Sea" (*Xi Hai*) in contrast to the "Eastern Sea," or China. Europeans were called "Western people" (*Xi ren*) and European missionaries were called "Western scholars" (*Xi ru*), as opposed to "Chinese scholars" (*Zhong ru*).

The sharp division between China and the West is more appropriate to the period 1800–2000, when the disparities between these two regions were so great, than to the earlier period 1500–1800. Recent research has shown that, during the seventeenth and eighteenth centuries, the most advanced cartography (mapmaking) in nations like France, Russia, and Qing China was increasingly international in character. In light of this and other research, the term "early modern," which historians have applied to Western history of 1500–1800, is seen more and more as applicable to global (and not merely European and North American) processes.

During the period 1500–1800, the flow of influence between East and West was not constant. Rather, it ebbed and flowed. Furthermore, while the influence was never equal in both directions, there was always at least some influence flowing in both directions so that the movement was never entirely one way. Similar dynamics of cultural borrowing and assimilation were apparent in both directions, though the ideas borrowed from the other culture were oftentimes applied in very different ways. For example, while the Chinese Christian literati used Christianity to supplant Buddhist and Daoist influences in Confucianism, the philosophes of the European Enlightenment used Confucianism to supplant the miracles of Christianity with the rationality of natural religion. Whereas the three centuries 1500–1800 saw a stronger flow of influence from China to Europe, the following two centuries (1800–2000) reversed that current with a stronger flow of influence from the Western world of Europe and North America to China. From 1500 to 1800, missionaries to China carrying Christianity and Western learning met with small degrees of receptivity that were overshadowed by a larger rejection. Likewise, European admiration for China during these years gradually evolved into disillusionment.

We use the patterns that we see in history to make sense of the past. These patterns tend to be a mixture of what is objectively present in history and what we subjectively choose to focus on in the past. This is a dynamic tension because, as history unfolds, the relationship between the present and the past changes. The topics of the four main chapters of this book illustrate this tension as they explore (1) the Chinese acceptance of Western culture and Christianity, (2) the Chinese rejection of these elements, (3) the Western acceptance of Chinese culture and Confucianism, and (4) the Western rejection of these elements. While the symmetry of these chapter divisions is neater and more groomed than the turbulent stream of historical events,

Figure 1.1.   Confucius depicted as a scholar-sage, from the Jesuit publication *Confucius Sinarum Philosophus* (Paris, 1687). Courtesy of the Niedersächsische Landesbibliothek Hannover. This image was widely reproduced in Europe and epitomized the seventeenth- and eighteenth-century positive view of the Chinese.

Figure 1.2. "The Miracle Teapot," a Russian depiction of the Chinese circa 1901. Source unknown. The six soldiers in the teapot appear to represent the primary nations that contributed troops to the international force sent in 1900 to lift the Boxer siege of the foreign legations in Beijing. They are (left to right) the United States (?), France, Russia (wearing the distinctive Russian shapka), Japan, Germany, and England. However, Italy and Austria also contributed small contingents. This caustic image shows how negative the Western view of the Chinese had become in the nineteenth and twentieth centuries.

the symmetry does allow us to reveal the underlying reciprocal flow of influence between China and the West.

In Europe, the predominant view of the Chinese was captured in images that changed radically between the periods 1500–1800 and 1800–2000. The first Europeans (the Portuguese) to make contact with the Chinese during this period did so in the early 1500s. This first cycle probably ended with the British ambassador Earl George Macartney's famous embassy to the court of the Qianlong Emperor in 1793 and the death of the Qianlong Emperor in 1799. The second cycle could be marked as ending with China's absorption of the British Crown Colony of Hong Kong on 30 June 1997 and the Portuguese colony of Macau on 20 December 1999.

During the period 1500–1800, the predominant image of China was captured in the sagely Confucius (551–479 BC). The most famous depiction of the learned sage shows him standing amid a library filled with books. The image was first published in *Confucius Sinarum Philosophus* (*Confucius, Philosopher of the Chinese*) in Paris in 1687 and then reduplicated in slightly variant forms in European publications of that time (see figure 1.1). By contrast, one of the most common images of the period 1800–2000 was the hostile depiction of John Chinaman, a vicious-looking, pigtailed Chinese male with long nails, whose stereotypical image as a domestic cook led him in one striking illustration to be shown standing over a teapot containing Europeans (see figure 1.2). (Actually, long nails in China were the province of the upper classes rather than domestics.) The implications of uncivilized cannibalism could not have made a greater contrast with the earlier image of a supremely civilized Confucius. There is no doubt that both images were distortions, one an idealization, the other a pejorative stereotype, and yet both accurately reflected images of the Chinese that Europeans held at different times.

In 1895 the British poet Rudyard Kipling published his "Ballad of East and West" and immortalized its opening line: "Oh, East is East, and West is West, and never the twain shall meet." Kipling had a romantic view of imperialism, and although he was thinking mainly of India, his line of verse became a standard phrase for expressing a fundamental difference between East Asia and the western world of Europe and North America. This divide was partly racial and partly cultural, but it was based on the belief that China and the West were fundamentally different.

In a similar vein, what the historian Jonathan Spence calls a "cult of the Chinese exotic" emerged in late nineteenth-century France. Chinese grace and delicacy, sensitivity, and sensuality were extolled as part of a unique and fascinating realm being destroyed by the overweening materialism of the

West. This exotic vision of China was popularized by the novelist Pierre Loti (Julien Viaud, 1850–1923) and the poet and novelist Victor Segalen (1878–1919). In our own day, the treatment of China as postmodern "otherness" or alterity has been disseminated by the French philosopher François Jullien and numerous American academics. This view of China and the West as fundamentally different belongs far more to the period 1800–2000 than to the earlier period 1500–1800. For most of this earlier period, the biblical teaching on a single line of human descent from Adam and Eve and through Noah united people. Not until the "reason" of Enlightenment thinkers prevailed was humanity divided into four races based on skin color.

Until the Communists' "Liberation" of China in 1949, much of the borrowing from the West was widespread and experimental. After 1949, the borrowing was restricted to the communist theories of Karl Marx, as modified to fit the needs of a nonindustrialized land. After 1949, the Western world's image of China changed in content but remained negative in tone. John Chinaman was replaced by the hordes of Communists, epitomized either as an army of blue ants or Red Guards, who practiced an oppressive totalitarianism. Except for a few apologists of the political Left in the West, the Chinese Communists were feared but not admired.

The question of whether history repeats itself has been long debated and never conclusively answered. But even if history does not repeat itself in a comprehensive way, we tend to see recurring patterns in the past, and we draw meaning from them. Recent years have witnessed a major shift in how the Western world sees China. This new view is characterized by mutual respect rather than an attitude of superiority. To find a similar degree of respect for China in Western history, we must go back to the period 1500–1800. Ironically, what is further removed from the present (1500–1800) may contain more meaning and relevance than the more recent past (1800–2000). That is the subject of this book.

WORKS CONSULTED

Billeter, Jean François. *Contre François Jullien*. Paris: Editions Allia, 2006.

Chan, Albert. *The Glory and Fall of the Ming Dynasty*. Norman: University of Oklahoma Press, 1982.

Clyde, Paul H., and Burton F. Beers. *The Far East: A History of the Western Impact and the Eastern Response, 1830–1970*. Englewood Cliffs, N.J.: Prentice-Hall, 1971.

Cohen, Paul A. *China Unbound: Evolving Perspectives on the Chinese Past*. London: RoutledgeCurzon, 2003.

Dawson, Raymond. *The Chinese Chameleon: An Analysis of European Conceptions of Chinese Civilization*. London: Oxford University Press, 1967.

de Bary, Wm. Theodore. *The Unfolding of Neo-Confucianism*. New York: Columbia University Press, 1975.

Elvin, Mark. *The Pattern of the Chinese Past: A Social and Economic Interpretation*. Stanford, Calif.: Stanford University Press, 1973.

Fairbank, John K., ed. *The Chinese World Order: Traditional China's Foreign Relations*. Cambridge, Mass.: Harvard University Press, 1968.

Fairbank, John K., and Albert M. Craig. *East Asia: The Modern Transformation*. Boston: Houghton Mifflin, 1960.

Fairbank, John K., and Edwin O. Reischauer. *East Asia: The Great Tradition*. Boston: Houghton Mifflin, 1958.

Fitzgerald, C. P. *The Chinese View of Their Place in the World*. London: Oxford University Press, 1964.

Franke, Wolfgang. *China and the West: The Cultural Encounter, Thirteenth to Twentieth Centuries*. Translated by R. A. Wilson. New York: Harper & Row, 1967.

Hostetler, Laura. *Qing Colonial Enterprise: Ethnography and Cartography in Early Modern China*. Chicago: University of Chicago, 2001.

Lee, James Z., and Wang Feng. *One Quarter of Humanity: Malthusian Mythology and Chinese Realities, 1700–2000*. Cambridge, Mass.: Harvard University Press, 1999.

Levenson, Joseph R. *Confucian China and Its Modern Fate: A Trilogy*. Berkeley: University of California Press, 1958–1965.

Mackerras, Colin. *Western Images of China*. Hong Kong: Oxford University Press, 1991.

Marks, Robert B. *The Origins of the Modern World: A Global and Ecological Narrative from the Fifteenth to the Twenty-first Century*. 2nd ed. Lanham, Md.: Rowman & Littlefield, 2007.

Marx, Karl. *Marx on China, 1853–1860: Articles from the* New York Daily Tribune. London, 1951.

Mungello, D. E. "The First Great Cultural Encounter between China and Europe (ca. 1582–ca. 1793)." *Review of Culture* (Macau) 2nd ser., (English ed.) 21 (1994): 111–20.

Pan, Lynn. *Sons of the Yellow Emperor: A History of the Chinese Diaspora*. New York: Kodansha, 1994.

Rawski, Evelyn S. *The Last Emperors: A Social History of Qing Imperial Institutions*. Berkeley and Los Angeles: University of California Press, 1998.

———. "Presidential Address: Reenvisioning the Qing: The Significance of the Qing Period in Chinese History." *Journal of Asian Studies* 55 (1996): 829–50.

Spence, Jonathan. *The Chan's Great Continent: China in Western Minds*. New York: W. W. Norton, 1998.

Teng Ssu-yü and John K. Fairbank, eds. *China's Response to the West: A Documentary Survey, 1839–1923*. Cambridge, Mass.: Harvard University Press, 1954.

Tsien, Tsuen-hsuin. "Western Impact on China through Translation." *Far Eastern Quarterly* 18 (1954): 305–27.

Waley-Cohen, Joanna. *The Sextants of Beijing: Global Currents in Chinese History.* New York: W. W. Norton, 1999.

Wills, John E., Jr. *Pepper Guns and Parleys: The Dutch East India Company and China, 1622–1681.* Cambridge, Mass.: Harvard University Press, 1974.

2

CHINESE ACCEPTANCE
OF WESTERN CULTURE
AND CHRISTIANITY

JESUIT ACCOMMODATION

Europeans in the form of Franciscan missionaries appeared in China as early as the thirteenth century, but their numbers were too small and the communications between China and Europe were too insubstantial to constitute a genuine cultural encounter. Not until the early 1500s did the first substantive contact between China and the West begin when the Portuguese entered south China. The mere physical presence of foreigners will not guarantee a genuine encounter. A culture must get beyond the physically defensive reaction of driving the aliens away or the mentally defensive act of closing one's mind to strange ideas. A cultural encounter requires some degree of interaction. Frequent reference to the fabled insularity of the Chinese has obscured the fact that many Chinese did indeed respond to the information and teachings that these Europeans (mainly Christian missionaries) brought to China. Two important questions to answer are as follows: Why were Chinese interested in Western learning? And why did Chinese become Christians? Even though the total number of Chinese who participated in the encounter was small, the participants included some of the most creative thinkers of that time. To answer these questions, we must begin with those who brought Western learning and Christianity to China.

One of the results of the Protestant Reformation was that it stimulated a religious revival in the Counter-Reformation that led Catholic missionaries to dominate the Christian mission in China throughout the period 1500–1800. In fact, the first Protestant missionary, Robert Morrison of the London Missionary Society, did not arrive in Chinese territory (Macau) until 1807. Whereas the Protestant Reformation (Lutheranism, Calvinism, and Anabaptism) dealt extensively with reforming religious teachings, Protestants

17

were very slow to send missionaries to far-flung regions of the world, such as China. Dutch Calvinists sought their personal fortune in trading with East Asia in the seventeenth and eighteenth centuries but made little attempt to missionize the people there. By contrast, although the Catholics refused to change their theology to accommodate the Protestants, they were inspired by the Protestant challenge to reform their hearts and practices. Whereas the Calvinist notion of a predestined elect seems to have discouraged missionary work, the Jesuit emphasis on free will in matters of salvation had the opposite effect. The Jesuits sought to carry God's word to the farthest reaches of the world and to give all human beings the opportunity to hear the Gospel and make a choice.

In the enthusiasm generated by the Counter-Reformation and to compensate for losses to Protestantism in Europe, dedicated Catholic missionaries were sent out on the newly established trade routes throughout the world. The Society of Jesus was founded in 1540 to assist the pope in countering the Protestant challenge. Jesuits took a special vow of loyalty to the pope. They became leaders in world missions and dominated the Christian mission in China during the period 1500–1800. While a number of Catholic groups (Franciscans, Dominicans, Augustinians, Jesuits, the Society of Foreign Missions of Paris, the Congregation for the Propagation of the Faith, and others) sent missionaries to China, the names of Jesuits became most famous. The striking achievements of these Jesuits have attracted the attention of historians to such an extent that the role of non-Jesuit Catholic missionaries in China has been slighted.

The founder of the Jesuit China mission was Francis Xavier (1506–1552), a Spaniard who visited Japan and the East Indies and who wished to enter China. Although he never penetrated the Chinese mainland and died on the offshore island of Shangchuan in 1552, his efforts were an inspiration to later Jesuits. Of these Jesuits, none is more famous than the Italian Father Matteo Ricci, S.J. (1552–1610), who is widely known to the Chinese as Li Madou. Perhaps the most brilliant of a group of Jesuits characterized by brilliance, Ricci arrived in Macau in 1582 and became one of the founders of the modern mission.

A gifted linguist, Ricci used the mnemonic (memory) techniques of Europe to impress the Chinese literati with their potential as a tool to memorize the Confucian classics. The practical value of such a tool in China cannot be overemphasized since nearly all paths to status and success lay through passing the civil service examinations that were based on memorizing the classics. Ricci also used European cartography to appeal to the literati by producing a world map with all the place-names given in Chinese. This famous map caused quite a stir among Chinese. Its use of Jesuit accommodation was shown in placing China near the center of the map, thereby accommodating the Sinocentric view of their country as the Middle Kingdom (*Zhongguo*). In 1601, after nineteen years of effort (including the clever use of European curiosity pieces, such as a self-striking clock and a clavichord), Ricci had attained the remarkable achievement of securing permission from the imperial government to establish a missionary residence in the capital of Beijing.

Although not the first Jesuit to enter China, Ricci was a pioneer in formulating the Jesuit missionary approach to China. Ricci's attitude toward Chinese culture and society was a relatively balanced mixture of praise and criticism. He admired the enormous size of China and its populace, the diversity of its crops, its favorable climate, the industry of its people, and its Confucian morality. But he was especially critical of Buddhist and Daoist monks whose personal and sexual immorality was flagrant. He was highly critical of Chinese sensuality and slavery, which he felt were related. And he reflected the homophobia of the Counter-Reformation Church in reserving his harshest criticisms for homosexual practices, particularly sodomy, which he described as widely practiced among Chinese males.

Jesuit accommodation was developed in close collaboration with Chinese literati to meet the unique demands of the mission field in China. Although Jesuit missionary policy as a whole stressed the accommodation of Christianity to indigenous elements of a foreign culture, nowhere had European missionaries encountered such an advanced culture as in China. This forced them to make difficult choices about what to accept and what to reject. If they accepted elements of Chinese culture that contradicted the Christian faith, the accommodation would become theologically invalid. If, on the other hand, they did not accept certain essential elements in Chinese culture, then the Chinese would reject Christianity as foreign and alien. If Christianity were to thrive in China, it would have to be inculturated there. This meant that it would no longer be seen as an exotic, foreign religion and instead would become not only something familiar but also a force that transformed Chinese culture.

The Chinese response to Christianity was clearly divisible along class lines between the literati and the common people. The literati received the most respect and prestige of any group in traditional Chinese society. Their status was based, at least in theory and to a large extent in reality, upon the egalitarian principle of education. Intensive study of the Confucian classics was aimed at preparing one for the official examinations. Success in the examinations on three ascending levels—somewhat comparable to the bachelor's, master's, and doctoral degrees—brought the immediate rewards of social prestige and certain legal privileges, such as exemption from physical abuse at the hands of scholar-officials. (The Chinese legal system contained no presumption of innocence of an accused individual, and corporal punishment was commonly used to extract confessions.)

In the long run, success in the examinations brought social prestige and official appointment that enabled one to participate in networks of enormous political and social influence and to obtain financial rewards from holding office. These financial rewards were usually invested in farmland—oftentimes managed by a clan (extended family)—that provided a financial return as well as refuge in the event of dismissal from office. As a result, there was considerable overlap between scholar-officials and landowning gentry.

In the period 1500–1800 these scholar-officials identified with the teachings of Confucius. Although they might participate in Buddhist and Daoist practices, such as using Buddhist monks for funerals or Daoist techniques to prolong their lives, Confucianism became the philosophy associated with wealth, status, and power. The poor, by contrast, were more likely to find refuge in Buddhism and Daoism. The poor often joined socially destitute gangs, such as secret societies, that blended Buddhist, Daoist, and other popular religious elements with illegal activities to scrape out a bare subsistence.

When the Jesuits first attempted to establish a residence in south China, they adopted the robes of the Buddhist monks, but the Jesuits soon realized their error and chose Confucianism rather than Buddhism as the basis for accommodation. This choice was understandable, given the cultural and social affinities of the highly educated Jesuits (many of whom also came from prominent families in Europe) with the highly educated and socially prestigious Chinese literati. Buddhist monks, who had declined in ability and social status from earlier periods, were criticized by the Jesuits for their intellectual superstitions, immoral practices, and social coarseness, while the literati were praised for their refinement and emphasis on learning. In addition, the literati presented a highly attractive power base to the Jesuits, who were accustomed in Europe and elsewhere to working close to the apex of the power structure. Moreover, a degree of tacit acceptance by the scholar-officials was necessary if the missionaries were legally to remain in China.

JESUIT CONVERSIONS OF THE LITERATI

In the early years of the mission, particularly in the more open cultural atmosphere of the late Ming, the Jesuits achieved remarkable success in converting prominent scholar-officials. This success came through the conscious blending of Confucianism with Christianity while criticizing Buddhism and Daoism. This attempt had first been formulated by Ricci and other Jesuit pioneers in China and was continued by the Jesuits throughout most of the seventeenth century. The most prominent of this first generation of converts were Yang Tingyun (1557–1627), Li Zhizao (1565–1630), and Xu Guangqi (1562–1633). These three were regarded as the Three Pillars of the early Christian Church. Xu was a first grand secretary, perhaps the highest official position in the Ming dynasty, and Li and Yang also occupied important positions.

Although the Three Pillars were all eminent scholar-officials who had studied the Confucian classics in order to pass the official examinations, their individual paths to Christianity differed. Xu was the first to be baptized (1601 in Nanjing), followed by Li Zhizao (1610 in Beijing) and Yang Tingyun (1611 in Hangzhou). All three remained committed to Confucian values, although Li was critical of Neo-Confucianism. Prior to their baptisms, their interest in Buddhism had varied; Yang was probably the most interested. After their baptisms, all three became harsh critics of Buddhism. Intellectually, all three harmonized Christianity with Confucianism.

However, a religious conversion is not a purely intellectual experience, and at least two of the Three Pillars underwent religious experiences that were crucial to their decision to be baptized. The personal crisis of failing the highest level of examination (the doctoral-level or *jinshi* exam) in 1597 made Xu Guangqi receptive to receiving instruction from the Jesuit fathers in 1598. This failure also probably saved him from taking a concubine, which was part of the standard celebratory practices of having arrived at this elevated status. In 1600, shortly after meeting Ricci, Xu had a dream of a temple with three chapels. The first chapel contained a shrine to God, the second a shrine to the son, and the third was empty. Much later Xu realized that this was a dream of the Trinity (Father, Son, and Holy Spirit). After failing the jinshi examination for a second time, Xu was deeply moved by a painting of the Madonna and Child and shortly thereafter was baptized.

Although Li Zhizao was much influenced by the mathematics and astronomy that Ricci taught, he was even more influenced by Ricci's character. Li had the closest relationship to Ricci of any of the Three Pillars, but his reluctance to send away his concubine was the final obstacle to his baptism. The practice of concubinage presented one of the greatest obstacles for literati wishing to be baptized. Affluent Chinese males took additional wives, or concubines, for reasons both sexual and familial. Such concubines often provided children of genealogical descent when the first wife could not procreate. Procreating the next generation, especially sons, was a matter of supreme importance to ancestor-revering Confucians. Although the status of a concubine was often precarious and below that of a wife, the concubine was legally and emotionally part of the family. Dismissing a concubine in order to be baptized as a Christian seemed harsh and notably contradictory for a religion that claimed love and mercy as its greatest virtues. Nevertheless, monogamy was a difficult matter for compromise in Christianity. Chinese who became Christians were forbidden to sell their daughters into servitude or concubinage.

Finally, Li experienced the personal crisis of a very serious illness in Beijing in early 1610; unattended by relatives, he was personally nursed for weeks by Ricci. At what appeared to be the point of death, he accepted the Christian faith and was baptized by Ricci. Li recovered soon thereafter; Ricci died in May of that year. In 1611 Li resigned from official duty and returned to his home in Hangzhou to care for his father, who was ill, inviting the Jesuits Lazzaro Cattaneo (1560–1640) and Nicolas Trigault (1577–1628) to accompany him.

Yang Tingyun's conversion was much less influenced by Ricci than was Li's. Yang met Ricci in Beijing, possibly in 1602, but did not become seriously interested in Christianity until almost a decade later. In 1609 he resigned his official post and retired to his home of Hangzhou. When he visited Li's home to express his condolences on the death of Li's father, he met Fathers Cattaneo and Trigault. He began serious discussions with them about Christianity and, after a long internal struggle, became a Christian. He first had to resolve serious questions about the veneration of the Buddha, the Incarnation of God in Jesus, and Christian redemption. Finally, he had to take the extremely difficult step of sending his concubine, who had given him two sons, to a separate dwelling. At one point, he was moved by a pictorial image of Christ. Although it is difficult to know the exact motive that led Yang to be baptized, it is clear that he differed from Xu and Li in not being drawn to Christianity because of either a personal crisis or admiration for Western science and mathematics.

The culture of the late Ming dynasty that the Christian missionaries encountered in China was experimental and had a looser sense of Confucian orthodoxy than other periods of Chinese history. Many late Ming literati were radical in their willingness to synthesize various teachings into a harmonious unity. The willingness of Ming culture to minimize differences and emphasize similarities was revealed in works like the famous novel *Journey to the West* (*Xi yu ji*)—also known as *Monkey*—by Wu Cheng'en (ca. 1500–1582). In this novel and throughout Ming culture, the teachings of

Confucianism, Buddhism, and Daoism were blended in syncretic unity under the often quoted phrase "The Three Teachings are really one." Such a blending would have been unthinkable in other periods of Chinese history when the exponents of these respective teachings competed and clashed with one another in their search for truth and imperial favor.

While the Jesuits refused to accept the blending of these three particular teachings, they did use the syncretic spirit of the Ming. However, instead of blending Buddhism and Daoism with Confucianism, the Jesuits sought to blend Christianity with Confucianism. They did this by attempting to displace Buddho-Daoism with Christianity and to create a Confucian-Christian synthesis. The eminent convert Xu Guangqi helped to shape this approach and expressed it with the famous phrase that Christianity should "supplement Confucianism and displace Buddhism" (*bu Ru yi Fo*). Whereas Confucianism was essentially a moral and social teaching that spoke only implicitly of spiritual forces, Buddhism spoke specifically and in great detail on spiritual matters. Confucianism's relative silence on spirits made it less vulnerable to criticism as a pagan religion, and its emphasis on moral and spiritual cultivation was viewed as reconcilable with Christianity's explicit treatment of spiritual forces and one God. Furthermore, the Chinese emphasis on filial piety echoed the biblical command to honor one's parents, and Confucius's formulation of the Golden Rule of treating others as one wished to be treated was very similar to what Jesus expressed in Matthew 7:12.

Later literati converts, such as Shang Huqing (ca. 1619–after 1698) of Jinan in Shandong province and Zhang Xingyao (1633–after 1715), baptized Ignatius, of Hangzhou, were less prominent. Shang and Zhang were thoughtful men who carried to deeper levels the attempt to reconcile Confucianism with Christianity. Furthermore, Shang and Zhang, in typical literati fashion, saw themselves in a tradition of Confucian-Christian literati of which Xu Guangqi was the founding master. They both advanced Xu's formula, "supplement Confucianism and displace Buddhism."

Shang had the unique experience of collaborating with both a Jesuit and a Franciscan in Jinan, in spite of the more typical hostility between Jesuit and non-Jesuit missionaries in China. During the years 1650–1665, Shang collaborated with Father Antonio Caballero a Santa Maria, O.F.M. (1602–1669), to produce works in Chinese on Christianity. Typical of these was *Confucianism and Christianity Compared* (*Tian Ru yin*), in which passages from the Confucian Four Books were cited to show the similarities between the two teachings. Shang also wrote a lengthy manuscript entitled "A Warning on Supplementing Confucianism" (*Bu Ru wengao*; 1664), which was never published. Several statements from this work reveal how unchauvinistic Shang's outlook was; for example, "People of the Eastern Sea [China] and Western Sea [Europe] live in different lands but under the same Heaven. They speak different languages but live by the same principles."

In 1702, after extensive study of Chinese history and the Confucian classics, Zhang Xingyao refined Xu's formula of supplementing Confucianism and displacing Buddhism into a three-part formula (harmonize, supplement, and transcend) to explain the similarities and differences between Confucianism and Christianity. In the first part, Zhang assembled numerous quotations from the ancient Chinese classics to show that Christianity and Confucianism were in agreement. In the second part, Christianity supplemented Confucianism in spiritual and moral cultivation as well as in other areas. In the third part, Christian revelation transcended the teaching of Confucianism. Zhang, too, voiced remarkably unchauvinistic sentiments. In the preface to a work entitled *Clearly Distinguishing the Heavenly Teaching [i.e., Christianity] [from Heterodoxy]*, he wrote, "In the Eastern Sea and the Western Sea sages arise who are identical in thinking." What is even more significant about this statement is that Zhang is quoting from the famous Neo-Confucian philosopher Lu Xiangshan (1139–1193). This indicates that Zhang saw himself not as an original thinker but rather in the model of Confucius, a transmitter of the wisdom of antiquity. Clearly, Zhang saw his acceptance of Christianity as within the orthodox tradition of Confucianism, even if he appeared to be a voice in the wilderness.

The development of these insights was the result of extensive collaboration between the missionaries and the literati who were sympathetic to Christianity. The Jesuits tended to write collaboratively in a way that obscured individual authorship. Furthermore, they were often hesitant to identify the role of Chinese collaborators because of hostile critics who would have eagerly exploited such identifications as evidence of heterodox sources in Jesuit writings. Chinese literati also had a tradition of collaborative authorship. Consequently, it is often very difficult to identify specific Jesuits and, even more so, Chinese literati who contributed to a particular work.

The Jesuit approach in missionizing was to work from the top down in converting social classes. In China, the highly educated Jesuits—the Society of Jesus is unsurpassed among Catholic religious orders in the effort it spends in educating its members—found their social and intellectual counterparts in the Confucian literati. Consequently, Ricci had a rapport with Xu Guangqi that enabled them to work closely together. After Ricci, the second most influential Jesuit was Giulio Aleni, S.J. (1582–1649). Father Aleni's abilities and achievements as a China missionary rank very close to those of Ricci, but while Ricci focused on the major cities like Nanjing and Beijing, Aleni worked in the more remote areas of southeast China, particularly in Fujian province. He had contact with numerous minor literati, one hundred of whom recorded his conversations, stories, and sermons from the decade 1630–1640. These were collected in chronological order by the Christian literatus Li Jiubiao (d. 1647) into a work entitled *Diary of Oral Admonitions* (*Kouduo richao*). These records were based on two hundred different meetings in ten coastal towns in Fujian, and they show that many Chinese literati assimilated the basic ideas of Christianity.

However, after the Manchu conquest of the native Chinese dynasty in 1644 and the founding of the Qing dynasty, the cultural atmosphere in China became less open to foreign influences, and the status of the literati converted by the Jesuits dropped, so that converts were those with lesser degrees and prestige, such as Shang Huqing, Zhang Xingyao, Zhu Zongyuan (ca. 1626–1666), and Qiu Sheng (before 1663–after 1706).

The success of missionizing a nation from the top down depended upon obtaining conversions among the most powerful and influential people so that they could influence lesser individuals to follow their example. As the status of the literati converts dropped, the Jesuit effort began to falter. But the process of assimilating Christianity in China did not stop. It continued to ebb and flow down through the years, undergoing a gradual shift from European to (after 1949) Chinese leadership.

CHRISTIANITY AS A SUBVERSIVE SECT

Missionaries of other religious orders in China aimed their work at a constituency very different from that of the Jesuits. Franciscans, particularly Spaniards, came from a culture that had been deeply influenced by the Reconquista by which Muslims and Jews in Spain had been forcibly converted to Christianity or expelled. Rather than seek accommodation as did the Jesuits, the Franciscans were stimulated by opposition. The Franciscan missionaries in China were energized by seeing their community of Christians as an island of believers surrounded by a sea of hostility. Inspired by the model of their founder, Saint Francis of Assisi, the Franciscan missionaries in China emphasized submission and martyrdom, both in their own training and in their apostolate.

The Franciscans aimed their missionizing at less prestigious groups in China. Writing in 1656, Father Antonio Caballero stated that his conversions in Shandong province (see map 2) had been entirely limited to the humblest and poorest people. He had failed to convert a single literatus during the preceding six years. Caballero expressed his frustration in dealing with wealthy people and merchants who showed little interest in religion. And yet, during his fifteen-year apostolate (1650–1665) in Shandong, Caballero baptized five thousand of these humble people. While the Franciscan missionaries did not ignore the need to cultivate the scholar-officials for political purposes, nearly all of their baptisms were among the lower social orders. The social and class antagonism in China at that time was expressed by the upper classes (literati) often being anti-Buddhist and anti-Daoist and by the lower classes (shopkeepers, craftsmen, peasants, workers, and the homeless) being anti-Confucian. Consequently, religious and class antagonism came together to reinforce one another in a way that would foster conflict with the Chinese government.

The missionaries promoted the development of confraternities, or religious brotherhoods and sisterhoods that were voluntary associations for the laity. These confraternities performed acts of Christian charity, assisted in funerals, taught catechism, and gathered abandoned and mortally ill children in order to baptize them into a state of grace before they died. In China there were separate confraternities for men (named for the Passion of Our Lord Jesus Christ), women (named for the Holy Virgin), children (named for Saint Agnes), students (named for Saint Louis of Gonzaga), literati (named for Saint Ignatius), and catechists (named for Saint Francis Xavier). Catechists played an important role in the Chinese church and often served as the head of the local church when a priest was absent.

The Confraternity of the Passion consisted of men who met to meditate on the sufferings of Christ at the time of his crucifixion. They observed penitential practices, such as fasting, wearing constraining fetters on their shoulders and arms, and self-flagellation, which was referred to as the "discipline." Much of this flagellation was done in secrecy, but there are records from the early 1700s of a Confraternity of the Passion meeting after mass on the third Friday of the month in a darkened and quiet atmosphere in the East Church of Jinan in Shandong province. Each member of the confraternity came forward to kiss the image of the crucified Lord Jesus then flagellated himself. In doing so, the men were attempting to imitate the flagellation Jesus had received just prior to his crucifixion. Their intention was to draw blood as a means of washing their souls clean of sin. Although the focus on the Crucifixion was new to China, this ascetic practice had native Chinese parallels in Daoist self-slapping (*zibo*) and Buddhist self-beating (*zipu*).

Because of the hostility that surrounded the Christians, the Franciscans resorted to secret meetings of their followers as a necessary expedient in circumventing the official prohibitions against their teachings. (One notes parallels to an underground Christian church—with an unofficial Catholic hierarchy and unregistered Protestant house churches—in contemporary China.) Secret meetings by Christian lay groups, such as the Confraternity of the Passion, may have been necessary, but they were also dangerous because they reinforced a link between Christianity and heretical, subversive societies, such as the White Lotus Society. The White Lotus Society was not a unified organization but rather a loosely used name for numerous peasant groups that engaged in illegal activities and shared a quasi-Buddhist teaching. (In Buddhism, the lotus is the symbol of rebirth from mud into a state of pure enlightenment.)

Secret societies have a nearly two-thousand-year history in China. They are linked to peasant uprisings, for which the societies provided an organization and ideology. The uprisings were nearly always aimed at the scholar-gentry class, who were viewed by the peasants as their oppressors because they controlled both the land and the government bureaucracy. Because of this intense hostility, the secret societies were viewed with suspicion and enmity by the scholar-officials. Like the secret societies, Christianity was often accused by the literati of subversive practices, such as prohibiting ancestor worship, meeting in small groups, using magical techniques to control followers, deceiving the people, and failing to observe customary distinctions of age and sex. Secret societies were criticized as hotbeds for dissolute intermingling of men and women.

These criticisms were not based on mere suspicion. After the lapse of conversions of eminent figures, Christianity found its greatest following among the same lower social classes who joined the secret societies. Not only did Christianity and the White Lotus Teaching draw many of their followers from the same lower classes, but also some individuals claimed to be adherents of both teachings at the same time. Certain White Lotus adherents in Shandong around 1700 even called their teaching by the same name as Christianity, "Lord of Heaven Teaching" (*Tianzhujiao*). By claiming membership in both teachings, the members of the White Lotus sect were able to circumvent the governmental prohibition against their sect and obtain the less restrictive prohibitions applied to Christianity. (Christianity had been awarded greater freedom by the Kangxi Emperor's Toleration Edict of 1692 and by other favorable imperial rulings obtained largely as rewards to the Jesuits for their service to the throne.) Some of the missionaries who were unfamiliar with Chinese society and driven by the desire to increase the number of converts agreed to baptize them. This created Christians whom the Confucian literati could rightly attack as heterodox. The anti-Confucian attitudes of the lower classes, along with their tendency to indiscriminately mix with members of quasi-Buddhist and quasi-Daoist secret societies, made them an object of official repression that would spill over to Chinese Christians.

CHINESE RITES CONTROVERSY FROM
THE CHINESE PERSPECTIVE

Once the Jesuits had chosen to concentrate on converting the Chinese literati as the first step toward converting the entire society, certain crucial problems had to be resolved. These included the choice of a Chinese name for the Christian God and how to interpret the rites performed to honor Confucius and familial ancestors. Was it permissible, these early Jesuits wondered, to use ancient Chinese terms such as *Shangdi* (Lord-on-High) or *Tian* (Heaven) to refer to God? Or were these terms too tainted with pagan associations in the minds of the Chinese to convey Christian concepts accurately? If so, was it then possible to coin a new Chinese word, *Tianzhu* (Lord of Heaven), or was it necessary to develop a Chinese transliteration for the name of God, such as *De-u-se* for Latin *Deus* (God)?

In regard to the crucial matter of rites, were the Chinese rites dedicated to Confucius and to ancestors acts of worship? Did they constitute petitions for blessings, or were they expressions of civil respect, social honor, and filial piety? These issues, which became part of the Chinese Rites Controversy, went to the very heart of the missionary effort because they required Europeans to separate what was truly essential to the Christian faith from what was merely cultural and secondary. The challenges that Christianity posed to Chinese converts involved the effort to reconcile with the Confucian tradition Christian ideas such as the Creation, Incarnation (of God in the human form of Jesus), Crucifixion, and Resurrection.

Chinese literati played an important role in the introduction of Christianity to China in the seventeenth and eighteenth centuries. However, their contributions were not fully appreciated because, aside from certain sympathetic Jesuits, most missionaries and church officials in Rome showed an inflexibility toward adapting Christianity to Chinese culture. Their inflexibility stemmed from their erroneous belief that the Europeanized church was a universal form for Christianity. The Chinese literati challenged this viewpoint. Chinese literati served as collaborators in the composition of major Jesuit works, such as Ricci's work *The True Meaning of the Lord of Heaven* (*Tianzhu shiyi*; 1603), but they also composed their own essays that presented the Chinese perspective in rebuttal to European interpretations. Many of these recently rediscovered essays have been preserved in Jesuit archives and libraries in Rome, Shanghai, and Beijing. These differences were incorporated into what is called the Chinese Rites Controversy.

Zhang Xingyao of Hangzhou was typical of this group of accommodationist literati; he composed an essay entitled "On the Ritual of Sacrifice" (*Sidian shuo*) around 1705. He conceded that certain sacrifices should be discontinued as un-Christian. However, discontinuing the use of ancestral tablets and rites to ancestors would cause Chinese Christians to be attacked by the rest of Chinese society as unfilial. Zhang and other Christian literati argued that rites to Heaven, ancestors, and Confucius were too ingrained in Chinese culture to abandon them. Instead, he proposed that these rites be reinterpreted; for example, rites to Heaven should be refocused on the monotheistic God of Christianity, while rites to ancestors and Confucius should be seen as forms of reverence rather than petitions or prayers.

Rites Controversy debate was most intense in Fujian province where an active group of Christian literati debated with a combative Catholic bishop named Charles Maigrot de Crissey (1652–1730). European missionaries divided largely on the lines of religious orders and nationalities. The Jesuits largely supported the Chinese while the Iberian mendicants (Dominicans and Franciscans) and secular priests were less accommodating. Bishop Maigrot was born and educated in Paris and joined the Society of Foreign Missions of Paris whose missionaries competed with the Jesuits in East Asia. Although Maigrot was resistant to any change in European Christianity, he realized the practical need to study the Chinese language and culture with the assistance of two low-level Chinese literati. Although his linguistic facility remained quite limited, it gave him a false confidence in his knowledge that would eventually cause him great embarrassment.

In his interpretation of the Chinese rites, Maigrot relied on the writings of a treatise written by the Dominican missionary Francisco Varo in 1672. Varo took a hard line in prohibiting Chinese Christians from performing ceremonies in honor of their ancestors and Confucius. The Christian literatus Yan Mo (baptized Paul) responded with an essay "Distinguishing Different Forms of Sacrifice" (*Bianji*) that defended the practice of Christians honoring their ancestors and Confucius. Yan argued that the word for sacrifice (*ji*) was ambiguous and that it meant different things when it was applied to sacrifices for ancestors, the ancient sages, primary teachers, and the Christian God. He emphasized that one needed to carefully distinguish the internal meaning from the outward ritual because the meaning of "sacrifice" varied with each case. If these different meanings were distinguished, it would become clear that no usurpation of God's authority occurred when Chinese performed the venerations to ancestors and Confucius. Maigrot, whose mind was closed to the Chinese point of view, regarded Yan's letter as an assault on his authority.

In 1693, one year after the Kangxi Emperor had issued his Edict of Toleration for Christianity, Maigrot took the confrontational step of issuing a mandate of seven prohibitions that were very hostile to the Chinese rites. Although Maigrot's prohibition applied only to the area of his jurisdiction (Fujian province in southeastern China), it inflamed an already delicate situation. Maigrot's opposition to allowing Chinese Christians to perform rites to ancestors and Confucius was based on his highly debatable interpretation of Confucianism. With the assistance of his two Chinese literati, Maigrot compiled a list of passages from Neo-Confucian philosophers, and particularly from Zhu Xi (1130–1200), that were contradictory to Christianity. His list included the Diagram of the Supreme Ultimate (*Taiji tu*; see figure 3.1).

When the faithful gathered on Easter Sunday in 1695 at the church in Zhangzhou, the Dominican Father Magino Ventallol announced that Bishop Maigrot refused the sacraments to anyone who did not accept his mandate banning the Chinese rites. Yan Mo's nephew Michael had assisted in writing his uncle's essays. However, now Michael was ill and eager to take confession and receive the sacraments, but Ventallol refused him the sacraments until he broke with his uncle. This coercion generated anger and additional writings from Yan Mo and other literati criticizing Maigrot.

The rites issue proved to be the major obstacle to conversion by seventeenth- and eighteenth-century literati, and Maigrot stands out as its most contentious spokesman. He personified the Counter-Reformation rigidity of Europe that was so alien to the Chinese setting. Jesuits since Ricci had realized that European-style confrontation did not play well in China where differences tended to be resolved in a process of "talking into harmony" (*shuohede*). Unlike the Jesuits, Maigrot was not receptive to adapting to the Chinese style, even though he was in China and dealing with Chinese. His obliviousness in this led him to misinterpret Chinese acts of humility. In 1701 in Jiangle, the Christian literatus Qiu Sheng met with Maigrot and his interpreter, the Spanish Franciscan Diego de Santa Rosa, to express his disagreement over the Chinese rites. In an act of personal humility, Qiu knelt before Maigrot, asking that Maigrot pardon him because he was an ignoramus who did not understand what he was saying, but Maigrot and his interpreter, Father Santa Rosa, misunderstood this formal act of humility and interpreted it in a literal way.

Qiu Sheng (before 1663–after 1706), baptized Matthew, achieved the highest literati degree (jinshi) in 1706. He and his brothers had demonstrated their filial piety in following their father in becoming Christians. Qiu's family had been baptized by Jesuit missionaries who accepted an accommodating view of the Chinese rites. In rebuttal to Maigrot's claims, Qiu Sheng wrote a letter and a long essay that showed that the Neo-Confucian views, formulated about fifteen hundred years after the death of Confucius, were misinterpretations of the original philosophy that Confucius had derived from Chinese antiquity. Qiu wrote that Ricci had been correct when he wrote in his famous essay *The True Meaning of the Lord of Heaven* (*Tianzhu shiyi*) that the ancient views of the Chinese, including the ancient Chinese concept of God, were in harmony with Christianity. The ancient Chinese, like the Old Testament Hebrews, worshiped a monotheistic God but were not yet aware of the truths of revelation that came later with Jesus Christ. Qiu warned that missionaries should cease criticizing Chinese honors to Confucius and ancestors and the practice of revering Heaven. Instead they should focus on explaining the Incarnation and Crucifixion to Chinese because the Chinese found these concepts difficult to understand and they presented the greatest obstacles to becoming Christian.

Maigrot was not receptive to any of these arguments. His intellectual rigidity eventually led to embarrassment at the highest level. Two Manchu officials sent by the Kangxi Emperor to interview him corrected his erroneous belief that the Supreme Ultimate had been part of ancient Confucianism, explaining that it had been developed much later by the Neo-Confucians of the Song dynasty (960–1126). In 1706 Maigrot was summoned to Manchuria for a personal interview with the Kangxi Emperor. The emperor became irritated when Maigrot could not support his rigid opposition to Chinese rites with even the most elementary ability to read Chinese classical texts. Maigrot was forced to concede in front of the emperor that he had never read Ricci's book *The True Meaning of the Lord of Heaven*, in which the distinction between ancient Confucianism and Neo-Confucianism was made. A few months later the emperor expelled Maigrot from China and ordered that only missionaries who accepted the accommodating views of Ricci would receive a permit (*piao*) to reside in China.

Jesuit accommodation, with its inherent sympathy and respect for Chinese culture and its willingness to collaborate with Chinese literati, tended to tolerate many indigenous Chinese cultural elements in deciding these questions, but this produced a negative reaction among many European Christians. Even some Sinologists have questioned whether the Jesuits' synthesis went so far in accommodating Confucianism that it resulted in a diluted form of Christianity, which the Dutch Sinologist E. Zürcher has called "Confucian monotheism." In spite of this degree of accommodation, the Jesuits faced enormous resistance to Christianity from the Chinese. The concept of a heavenly God had a close counterpart in Confucianism. The notion of an afterlife with experiences in heaven and hell had already been introduced into China by Buddhism, although not all literati accepted these concepts. The Creation was a new idea in China, but even that did not provoke the greatest resistance. It was, as Qiu Sheng noted, the Incarnation and Crucifixion of Christ that the literati most resisted. In Chinese society, which made sharp social distinctions on the basis of whether one worked with one's hands or one's mind, the literati earned exemption from most forms of corporal punishment. By contrast, brutal punishment of the lower classes was commonplace in China. It was very difficult for the literati to accept that the incarnation of God on Earth would submit to such a degrading lower-class punishment as crucifixion.

Because of the negative reaction of literati to the Incarnation and Crucifixion, Ricci and later Jesuits delayed presenting these fundamental teachings in religious instruction to prospective converts. Other groups of missionaries, such as the Franciscans, whose apostolate was primarily among the lower classes, taught the Incarnation and Crucifixion more openly. The Jesuits could scarcely display the crucifix because it was perceived as a form of black magic aimed at the person of the Chinese emperor and consequently evoked intense hostility. Nevertheless, the Jesuits did teach the Incarnation and Crucifixion, as is clearly shown by Father Aleni's adaptation of Gerónimo Nadal's famous illustrated life of Christ discussed below and depicted in figure 2.4. However, because of its sensitivity, the Jesuits tended to reserve the Crucifixion as one of the last teachings to be imparted to converts.

THE CLOSING OF CHINESE MINDS (CA. 1644)

After the Manchu conquest of 1644, Chinese resistance to foreign influences increased. Such a resistance was not typical of Chinese history. During the seven centuries from AD 200 to 900, China had been very open to foreigners and foreign influences. This was the age when monks from Central Asia brought Buddhism to China and when Chinese monks made long journeys to India to obtain Buddhist scriptures. This period culminated with the great age of the Tang dynasty (618–907), which was cosmopolitan, sophisticated, and largely acceptant of non-Han peoples, whether Turks from Central Asia or Muslim Arabs from the Indian Ocean region. The Chinese represent an ethnic (rather than a racial) group who share a culture. (Over 90 percent of the 1.3 billion people who live in China today are Han Chinese.) It is difficult to classify Chinese primarily in terms of physical characteristics. We can say that Han Chinese belong to what anthropologists have called the Mongoloid racial group, which includes the distinctive features of straight black hair, dark eyes, flat faces, epicanthoid folds (almond-shaped eyes), and a minimum of facial and body hair. But there are many non-Han Chinese with different physical characteristics.

Because of the physical differences between Han and non-Han Chinese, identity as a Chinese has traditionally been regarded as much a matter of culture as of race. This shared culture was based upon the written Chinese characters. However, with the founding of the Ming dynasty in 1368, the Chinese began a long, gradual process of turning inward (see chapter 1). This turning inward may have been due to political decisions by early Ming emperors, or it may have been due to the remarkable prosperity of the Ming dynasty. In any case, it strengthened and solidified feelings of Chinese ethnocentrism, which in its extreme forms produced chauvinism (feelings of superiority) and xenophobia (antiforeign feeling). Over the period 1500–1800 these feelings gradually increased and intensified. This process explains, in part, why Chinese literati were more receptive to Western influences during the earlier part of this period than the later part.

What is notable is that Chinese feelings of chauvinism and xenophobia lagged behind technological and economic realities by several centuries. China's science and technology peaked sometime in the mid-fourteenth century (approximately when the Ming dynasty was founded), when it became the world's most populous nation and the one with the highest rate of literacy. Creativity in science and technology began to falter, and China entered into a long and very gradual, almost imperceptible decline. It would take several centuries for this loss of intellectual creativity to translate into economic, military, social, and cultural decline. Moreover, the economic prosperity of the Ming served to mask the underlying scientific and technological stagnation. Chinese feelings of cultural superiority became so ingrained that foreigners would recognize the signs of decline before the Chinese themselves did. Lord Earl Macartney of Great Britain, during his embassy to the court of the Qianlong Emperor in 1793, was one of the first foreign observers to notice these signs of drift and lack of forward momentum. Meanwhile, the Chinese felt themselves to be living in a great golden age, without realizing that the glory belonged to an Indian summer rather than to summer's peak.

The position of Jesuit accommodation became less tenable after the Manchu invasion of 1644, as the Chinese reverted to a stricter sense of orthodoxy during the Qing dynasty. With the decline of the syncretic spirit in Chinese culture, the literati became less willing to accept the synthesis of Confucianism with a foreign religion. In fact, the literati became reluctant to accept the blending of Confucianism with any non-Confucian elements, including Buddhism and Daoism. There was a reassertion of the transmission of the Dao (Way or Truth) from the ancient sages through Confucius and his followers down to the present. There was little place in such a perspective for a foreign religion. This was the cultural current against which Jesuits of the late seventeenth and eighteenth centuries had to struggle, and it made conversions of eminent literati far more difficult than in earlier times.

Although cultural conditions in China became less fertile for Christianity, the Jesuits continued to find employment in prominent positions at the court. However, because they were occupied with the concerns of the court, their emphasis shifted away from the cultivation of the literati in the provinces. The continued prominence of the Jesuits during the late seventeenth century and throughout the eighteenth was indicative of the quality of the missionaries sent to China and the willingness of the Manchu emperors to make use of their services. Men like the German Johann Adam Schall von Bell (Tang Ruowang, 1592–1666) and the Belgian Ferdinand Verbiest (Nan Huairen, 1623–1688) would have been outstanding in practically any environment. Fathers Schall and Verbiest were the first Europeans to head the important Chinese Bureau of Astronomy, where the mathematically trained Jesuits held prominent positions for more than 150 years (see figure 2.1). When the Manchus conquered China in 1644 and established the Qing dynasty, the technical skills of the Jesuits enabled them to be retained at the Beijing court, smoothing the transition between political masters. Schall and Verbiest were also close to the Manchu emperors of China and had regular contact with them.

Schall established a particularly close relationship with the first Manchu ruler, the young Shunzhi Emperor (r. 1644–1661), who came the closest of any Chinese emperor to being baptized. The emperor was light skinned with dark hair, somewhat slight, but a good horseman in the Manchu manner. He was bright and studied hard to master the Chinese language. He was a conscientious ruler, decisive, with a strong interest in religion. During the first seven years after taking personal control of the government (1651–1657), he developed an unusually close and affectionate relationship with Schall, consulting him on affairs of state as well as religious matters. The emperor often called Schall to his imperial quarters, sometimes at night, or impulsively vis-

Figure 2.1. The ancient Beijing Astronomical Observatory of the Bureau of Astronomy, first built under the Mongols and located just inside the southeast portion of the Tartar City Wall. Although the wall has been dismantled, the observatory remains, located on Jiangguomenwai Avenue. The platform containing the astronomical instruments stands over forty-five feet (fourteen meters) in height. The Jesuit Father F. Verbiest took a leading role in the construction of these instruments circa 1673 and in the running of the observatory.

ited Schall at the mission residence near the palace. He was very informal with Schall, sitting cross-legged on Schall's bed and asking about Christianity and life in Europe. In fact, he called Schall by the affectionate Manchu name of *ma-fa* (grandpa), an indicator that this relationship between a teenager and a priest in his sixties was much like that of grandson and grandfather. The emperor was particularly fascinated by an illustrated life of Christ (probably based on Nadal's work) among Schall's books. When he came to the Crucifixion of Christ, he was so moved that he fell to his knees while Schall knelt beside him. The emperor also visited Schall's church and had Schall explain all the eucharistic vestments. The relationship between Schall and the Shunzhi Emperor was such that Schall could present his petitions directly to the emperor, bypassing the usual official screening process.

Schall's success aroused envy. The priest grew arrogant and lived in princely style apart from his confreres in a house given to him by the emperor. Criticisms were voiced, and some reached the level of scandal when

Schall was accused of breaking his priestly vow of chastity and having sexual relations with Chinese—both a man and a woman. The Portuguese Jesuit Gabriel de Magalhães (1610–1677), a vigorous defender of Portuguese interests in the China mission, accused Schall of indiscreet behavior (though not sodomy per se) in engaging in a homoerotic relationship with his manservant Pan Jinxiao. In returning from a banquet, Schall had Pan ride behind him (pillion style) on his horse, as was the custom among male lovers in China. Moreover, Schall was extremely solicitous of Pan, agreeing to his wishes in a way that was very odd by Chinese standards and raising eyebrows by adopting Pan's son, Pan Shihong. Finally, Pan criticized Schall in the manner of a spurned lover when he accused Schall of losing interest in him because he had found someone else. Although Schall did, on his deathbed, ask for his confreres' forgiveness for the excessive indulgence he showed to Pan and his son, historians have failed to find any firm evidence to support the rumors of a sexual affair.

Schall was such a monumental figure that accusations continued to surface long afterward. In 1758, nearly a century after Schall's death, an old accusation resurfaced that Schall had a sexual affair with a female servant in his house and fathered two children. Since the accusation was voiced by a secretary of one of the Jesuits' bitterest enemies, the papal legate and cardinal Thomas Maillard de Tournon, it is possible to dismiss the accusation as malicious gossip.

Although prospects for Schall's converting the emperor of China to Christianity looked favorable, the moment passed. The Shunzhi Emperor appears to have been very interested in sex and disinclined to accept Schall's admonitions about controlling his sex drives, which Schall called "lusts of the flesh." Moreover, the Jesuits' demand for strict adherence to monogamy conflicted with a Chinese emperor's duty to have an active sex life with multiple wives in order to produce an abundant supply of heirs to the throne. After 1658 the emperor turned increasingly to the more solicitous voices of eunuchs who encouraged him to indulge his desires while they increased their political power. His religious interests continued, but they moved in the direction of Chan (Zen) Buddhism. At any rate, the Shunzhi Emperor did not have a long life. Weakened by tuberculosis, he died of smallpox in 1661, one month short of his twenty-third birthday.

While Jesuit influence on the Chinese literati peaked in the late Ming between 1600 and 1644 (the year of the Manchu conquest), Jesuit influence on the Manchu rulers of China peaked in the early Qing dynasty between 1644 and 1705. The Jesuits had converted several prominent scholar-officials who assisted them. One of the most important officials of the Qing period, Wei Yijie (1616–1686), was a secret Christian. Although Jesuits continued to work at the court throughout the eighteenth century, their work as painters and architects appears to have given them a narrower craftsman status, which lowered their access to the throne.

Jesuit influence on the Chinese throne was aided by the missionaries' brilliance, training, and spiritual discipline, but it was hindered by a growing contentiousness. Not only did the Jesuits contend with other missionaries in the Rites Controversy and over other issues, but they also argued with one another. One of the greatest sources of conflict among the Jesuits themselves was based upon nationalistic differences. Out of 920 Jesuits who participated in the China mission between 1552 and 1800, 314, or over one-third, were Portuguese. Considering that Portugal had a population of only about one million people at that time, how do we account for this high proportion of Portuguese? In part, it was due to the Portuguese crown's support of Christian missions, and in part it was due to the *padroado* (a monopoly granted by the papacy over missionary and other activities in Asia).

The division of the world between Spain and Portugal explains why, until the end of the seventeenth century, there were only two official routes from Europe to China (see map 1). The shorter route involved obtaining a visa and passage out of Lisbon on Portuguese ships, which went round the southern Cape of Africa and landed at Goa in India. The traveler then obtained onward passage on Portuguese ships to Macau. The longer route involved departure from Seville on Spanish ships. After crossing the Atlantic to Mexico, one crossed Central America to Acapulco and took passage on a Spanish ship across the Pacific Ocean to the Philippines. Onward passage from the Philippines to China was fraught with difficulties because the Portuguese would arrest anyone who disembarked in Macau without a Portuguese visa. Consequently, the Spanish Franciscans tended to avoid Macau and land illegally on the coast of Fujian province in southeastern China.

While Spain produced many China missionaries, most of them were Franciscans and Dominicans rather than Jesuits. There were also many Italian Jesuits (ninety-nine) who served in China, but Italian identity was diluted by the fact that at that time Italian affiliations were regional rather than national. By the end of the seventeenth century, Dutch and French ships had broken the Portuguese monopoly on shipping routes to East Asia. Although the Dutch Calvinists would send no missionaries to China until after 1800, the large number of French Jesuits (130) reflected the emergence of France as a European power. The French Jesuits, like the French political leaders, were unwilling to honor the Portuguese monopoly, and this led to contention in China between Portuguese Jesuits, including Father Tomé Pereira

(1645–1708), who was a favorite of the Kangxi Emperor, and the French Jesuits, who were arriving in increasing numbers. This conflict diminished respect for the missionaries in the eyes of the Chinese.

Rome, recognizing that interorder and nationalistic rivalries were hindering missionary efforts throughout the world, tried to pacify the situation by creating a controlling body. The Sacred Congregation for the Propagation of the Faith, known as Propaganda, was created by papal decree in 1622, but it was frustrated in its efforts by the Portuguese monarch, who refused to relinquish the prerogatives of the padroado.

The intense interorder rivalries led to the use of secret codes in missionary correspondence. In 1601 the secretary to the Jesuit father-general sent out a letter to all provincials (heads of religious districts) of the Society of Jesus. The letter conveyed a new code that was to replace the old code and to be used until it was replaced by yet another code. In this new code, a two-digit number (from forty-one to sixty-two) was assigned to each of the twenty letters of the Latin alphabet (j, k, v, w, x, and y were omitted). In writing official correspondence, one was to use the assigned numbers in place of letters. In order to prevent decipherment, the numbers assigned to the alphabet changed with each letter. For example, *Papa* (pope) might be 47-49-55-55 or 42-54-55-55 or 46-41-47-49 or 55-55-42-54, depending on its position in the document; *fingido* (deceitful, two-faced) might be 61-58-44-47-42-53-45 or 55-41-53-62-58-57-54, and so on.

CHINESE REACTION TO
EUROPEAN TECHNOLOGY AND ART

The Jesuit motto "for the greater glory of God" (*ad maiorem Dei gloriam*) often appeared on the dedication page of Jesuit works published in the seventeenth and eighteenth centuries. Jesuits tried to glorify God not only in their lives but also in the artifacts they chose to carry from Europe to China.

In material history, clocks are microcosms of technological development. China had preceded Europe in AD 725 in creating the first mechanical clock to use escapement (the controlled release of energy in a timepiece). One of the most famous of early Chinese clocks was a ten-meter-high invention by Su Song in 1088, in which escapement was driven by scoop wheels using water. Not until the late thirteenth century did Europe create its first mechanical clock, which, instead of using scoop wheels of water, used a falling weight for escapement. The release of energy from the falling wheel was regulated by a verge-and-folio escapement in which the rotary motion of a wheel was converted into the vibratory motion of a balance that was used to measure time. By the sixteenth century, European clockmakers had developed the use of a pendulum, which added precision to timekeeping.

In the 1580s, Ricci and other missionaries began arriving in China with chiming clocks, referred to in China as *zimingzhong* (self-chiming bells). Because Chinese knowledge of horology had been lost over the years, these European mechanical clocks became objects of exotic fascination. Unlike early Chinese literati who were interested in European science and technology, most Chinese of the Ming and Qing periods saw European clocks not as timepieces but rather as decorative items and status symbols.

The Kangxi (r. 1661–1722) and Qianlong (r. 1736–1795) emperors were particularly interested in these clocks. The former had craftsmen from throughout China come to Beijing in an effort to duplicate the workshops the Jesuits said had been created by Louis XIV's Academy of Sciences in France. Hundreds of workers and craftsmen were employed, with European missionaries having prominent roles. While these imperial workshops in Beijing produced clocks for the court, the main center for the manufacture of clocks in China was far to the south, close to the port of Canton where most European ships unloaded their cargoes. The Chinese demand for clocks was strong enough to keep over a hundred clockmakers busy in Europe, making clocks in an imaginary Chinese style called *chinoiserie* (pronounced sheen-*waz*-eh-ree). The leading clock manufacturers were James Cox (d. ca. 1791) of London and Jaquet-Droz et Leschot of Switzerland. The Canton workshops imitated many of these European clocks, while the Beijing workshops excelled in producing the most authentic hybrid forms that blended European style with traditional Chinese motifs.

When the missionaries arrived in China, they brought works from one of the most magnificent achievements of Western art. Since the Renaissance, pictorial images had played an enormous role in European Christianity, and missionaries to China rightly saw them as important tools for teaching the Chinese about Christianity. Consequently, the first European works of art to arrive in China were devotional paintings, illustrated books, and engravings, many of which were devoted to biblical themes. They arrived on Portuguese and Spanish ships traveling from Europe to China.

The devotional oil paintings produced in the Renaissance fascinated the Chinese. Not only did the pictorial images foster conversions among Chinese, but also their lifelike quality caused the merely curious to flock to the Christian churches to view the Western pictures. Chinese were impressed by the Western use of three-dimensional space through the techniques of perspective and chiaroscuro. (Chiaroscuro [pronounced kee-ar-eh *skyoor'*-o] is a style of painting that uses only light and shade to attain a third dimension.) Western engravings and illustrated books also struck a responsive chord among the Chinese and were easily copied by Chinese wood engravers. These books were reproduced as part of the extensive Jesuit effort to translate European books into Chinese. By the end of the eighteenth century, over four hundred such translations had been produced in China.

Another feature of European art that was assimilated into Chinese culture was perspective. Prior to the Renaissance, Europeans used the word *perspectiva* (perspective) as part of the science of vision derived from Greek optics. However, in the early Renaissance, the term was redefined in a more specific way to refer to linear perspective and its application to painting. China missionaries regarded perspective as a deeply theological part of Euclidean geometry because they believed the presentation of things in geometrical forms revealed the orderly and logical principles on which God created the world. Consequently, China missionaries used perspective in their religious pictorial decoration as a liturgical and evangelical tool to attract Chinese to Christian churches.

The baroque style of painting was part of the Counter-Reformation response to the Protestant iconoclasm that had destroyed works of art in the churches. Baroque artists painted sacred images in an emotional and striking manner that would stimulate religious belief in Europe and conversions abroad. The famous treatise on perspective *Perspectiva Pictorum et Architectorum* (Rome, 1693–1701) by the Jesuit Andrea Pozzo was one of many scientific treatises translated into Chinese as a means of transmitting evangelical truths. The Kangxi Emperor's fascination with the technique of linear perspective caused a school of perspective to emerge at the imperial court under the leadership of the lay painter Giovanni Gherardini (1655–1723).

Gherardini was trained in Bologna in the school of *quadratura* (ornamentation in perspective of ceilings and walls). He was brought to Beijing by Father Joachim Bouvet in 1699, probably because of the frescoes he had produced in the Jesuit headquarters at Paris, which excelled in perspective. In Beijing in 1701–1703 Gherardini decorated the walls, ceiling, and cupola of the new European-style Jesuit Beitang (North Church) with frescoes of striking perspective that intrigued Chinese visitors. Gherardini modeled his work on the ceiling frescoes by the Jesuit painter Andrea Pozzo in the Church of St. Ignatius in Rome. In addition, he taught perspective and oil painting to Chinese students. But Gherardini was unhappy with the strictures of religious life in Beijing and remained for only five years before returning to France in 1704. The Kangxi Emperor was fascinated by his work and reluctant to let him go but eventually sent him off with a gift of one hundred taels (ounces) of silver.

Nevertheless, the effects of Gherardini's visit remained, and Father Matteo Ripa reported seeing seven or eight of Gherardini's students in 1715 painting Chinese landscapes in oils on sturdy Korean paper. Fathers Verbiest and Ludovici Buglio, S.J. (1606–1682), of Sicily were not artists but contributed by teaching perspective to Chinese students. The literati and the Kangxi Emperor were so fascinated by the artistic technique of drawing perspective that the Jesuits produced a Chinese adaptation of Pozzo's *Perspectiva Pictorum et Architectorum*. The Jesuit lay brother Giuseppe Castiglione (1688–1766) of Milan collaborated with the high official Nian Xiyao to produce this work intended primarily for Chinese painters, entitled *Visual Learning* (*Shixue*), in two editions, 1729 and 1735.

Nian Xiyao (1671–1738) was a prominent Chinese official who was fascinated by the mathematics (trigonometry) and linear perspective that the Jesuits taught. He met Gherardini and made contact with a number of his students as well as extensive contact with the Jesuit painter Giuseppe Castiglione (Lang Shining, 1688–1766), a coadjutor brother. Nian maintained extensive contact with a number of Jesuits who taught him trigonometry. Nian wrote prefaces for his two works (1729 and 1735) containing partial translations of Pozzo's work on perspective that he entitled "The Essence of the Science of Vision" (*Shixue jingyun*). These were studied by a number of Chinese painters.

In 1578 a group of Spanish Franciscans processed through Macau carrying a small print of the Virgin and Child after Saint Luke, copied from a work in the Church of Santa Maria Maggiore in Rome. However, when the Jesuits displayed a painting of the Virgin and Child at their residence in Zhaoqing near Canton, Chinese confused the Virgin with the Buddhist bodhisattva Guanyin. In Buddhism, a bodhisattva is characterized by compassion for the suffering of other sentient beings. Although enlightened, the bodhisattva delays entry into nirvana, instead seeking continued rebirth in the world of suffering in order to assist other human beings to attain enlightenment. Because Chinese women often prayed to the compassionate Guanyin for assistance in conceiving and bearing a child, preferably a boy, Guanyin is sometimes portrayed with a son in her arms. To eliminate this confusion, the Jesuits replaced the picture of the Virgin and Child with a painting portraying the theme *Salvator Mundi* (savior of the world), which typically shows the upper body of Christ, who is holding an orb and cross in one hand and blessing it with the other hand. The painting was by

Father Giovanni Niccolò (Cola), S.J. (1563–1626), of Naples, who arrived in Macau with Ricci in 1582.

Most of the artwork initially used by missionaries in China had been shipped from Europe. Although some of it had been produced by eminent European artists, it became clear that the iconographic needs of the missionaries could best be supplied by Chinese artists. In Manila, the Jesuit painter Father Antonius Sedeno ran a school for Chinese painters, supplying churches in the Philippines with devotional pictures in the Western style. Of more significance was the school for painters in Japan run by Father Niccolò. A school for copper engravers was established in Japan in the late sixteenth century.

The first Chinese artist to serve the Jesuits was the lay brother Yu Wenhui (alias Manuel Pereira), S.J. (1575–1633). Yu was born in Macau and was sent to study painting in Japan under Father Niccolò in the 1590s. Although his religious paintings were mediocre, Yu did assist Ricci on his deathbed in Beijing in 1610 and later painted the famous portrait of Ricci that hangs today in the sacristy of the Church of the Gesù in Rome. When Ricci complained of Father Yu's mediocrity as a painter, a second painter was sent to China from Father Niccolò's school in Japan. This painter, Ni Yicheng (alias Jacques Niva or Niwa), S.J. (1579–1638), was born in Japan to a Chinese father and a Japanese mother. He arrived in Macau in 1601 at eighteen years of age and thereafter divided his time between Macau, Nanchang, and Beijing. His religious paintings were in great demand by Chinese Christians. One of his paintings, or a derivative thereof, was a Chinese version of the Virgin and Child after Saint Luke in the Church of Santa Maria Maggiore in Rome.

Many of these Christian pictures presented in China depicted biblical events, particularly those of the Gospels. These biblical events and images of the Virgin Mary had been popular artistic themes among Renaissance and mannerist artists of Europe. These paintings were placed in Christian churches in China and attracted large numbers of interested Chinese. Unfortunately, very few of these early Christian paintings in China have survived. There were also court paintings portraying members of European royal families, such as Louis XIV of France, but these circulated only within the Chinese court.

What circulated to a far wider audience in China than the paintings were the illustrated books and loose sheets of engravings from Europe. These used techniques and pictorial elements that were more adaptable to Chinese ink painting and woodblock printing than the oil paintings of religious themes and European royalty. These illustrated books and engravings featured European landscapes and settings whose realism, perspective, shading, and chiaroscuro are said to have fascinated Chinese artists. Another influential European element was plasticity, the use of tonal contrasts and shadows to give the appearance of three-dimensionality rather than the three-dimensional space used by Chinese artists. Some of these elements had been introduced with Buddhist art a thousand years before but, after arousing some Chinese curiosity and imitation, had faded. Now these techniques, this time from Europe, were once again attracting attention in China. European engravings sent to China numbered at least in the hundreds and perhaps in the thousands. Some of these European illustrations and engravings were reproduced in Chinese works of art.

Among the first attempts to intermingle European and Chinese art, the most impressive was a work of illustrations on the life of Jesus produced by Father Giulio Aleni. In his effort to propagate Christianity in Fujian, Aleni used one of the most powerful tools that Europe was then producing: the vivid pictorial images of Renaissance artists, whose sacred images were received with respect and fascination in China.

In the early seventeenth century, the most famous illustrated version of the Gospels was the work *Images of the History of the Gospel* (*Evangelicae Historiae Imagines*; 1593) by Gerónimo Nadal, S.J. (1507–1580). Nadal's book combined 153 large engravings with written meditations in a manner influenced by *The Spiritual Exercises* of Saint Ignatius Loyola, the founder of the Society of Jesus. Nadal was so close to Loyola that he is referred to as Loyola's alter ego. In his famous spiritual manual, *The Spiritual Exercises* (1533), Loyola had developed the technique of using the senses (sight, hearing, smell, and touch) to reinforce Jesus' teachings. We see Nadal using this technique in combining these vivid illustrations with a written text to convey the life and teachings of Jesus. The use of these images to convey a faithful representation of Scripture was also a Catholic response to the Protestant demand for closer adherence to Scripture. Although the result has sometimes been criticized as being slavish to the printed word, at the time the work was produced, these illustrations were meant not only to narrate the events of Jesus' life but also to serve as a basis for biblical meditations. The use of visual images in mnemonic techniques was still common at that time, although the mnemonic tradition is practically forgotten today.

Because of fears of an examination by the Roman Inquisition, Nadal had not published his work before dying in 1580. The project was taken up by the Jesuit father general Claudio Acquaviva. The finest craftsmen in the art of copper engraving in seventeenth-century Europe were found in Antwerp and Amsterdam, and it was in Antwerp that the Jesuits tracked

現叠蹟靈釘被穌耶

甲耶穌高懸萬民仰此
受釘于十字架上

乙惟時遍物哀且日月
俺光渾天幽暗

丙同釘一盜愬耶穌
天主悔罪而卽蒙救

丁聖堂帳幔自裂顯露
內堂之奧

庚古塚自啟
辛兵將見諸靈異驚愕
讚嘆

壬惡黨亦知痛悔撫心

戊大地全震而山崩
巳石柱裂而石相擊

重首以歸
癸兵辛敲折二盜髀以
速其死

子耶穌旣沒一辛持戟
刺其右脇水血流出

丑聖母諸聖痛望諸狀
見行紀七卷三十四

Figure 2.2. The Crucifixion of Jesus Christ from G. Aleni, S.J., *Tianzhu jiang-sheng chuxiang jingjie* (Incarnation of the Lord of Heaven through Illustrations and Commentary; Hangzhou, 1637). Permission of the Archivum Romanum Societatis Iesu, Rome. Father Aleni's work is based upon the famous work *Evangelicae Historiae Imagines* (Antwerp, 1593), by Gerónimo Nadal, S.J.

像 架 刑 釘 方 穌 耶

第四十二圖

Figure 2.3. Driving spikes into the body of Jesus as part of the punishment of the Crucifixion. This illustration was originally one of forty-eight drawings on the life of Christ presented by Father J. Schall to the Chongzhen Emperor in 1640. Yang Guangxian used this illustration in his anti-Christian work *I Cannot Do Otherwise* (*Budeyi*; 1664) to attack Christianity by showing that Jesus was really an outlaw who was executed for the crimes of rebellion and sedition.

down their favorite engravers in the taverns. The talents of the Wierix brothers Antonius (1555–1603) and Hieronymous (1551–1614) as engravers were surpassed only by their debauchery, drunkenness, and greed for money. After many adjustments to the drawings and protracted negotiations, the Wierix brothers agreed to undertake the task. The production costs were enormous, but the work was finally printed in Antwerp in 1593 and was widely disseminated in Europe.

The publication of Nadal's work was eagerly anticipated by missionaries in East Asia, who as early as 1584 were sending letters to Rome requesting copies. The missionaries realized that holy pictures conveyed the mysteries of the Christian faith in ways that sometimes were more effective than words. In China during the late Ming dynasty there had been a proliferation of printing as an increasingly literate society demanded books in ever greater numbers. In China, unlike in Europe, both books and graphic art were printed with carved wooden blocks. The great demand for printed and graphic materials in China had brought graphic art to its peak of development around 1600. Graphic art, a popular medium, was widely employed to inform and to entertain.

By 1605 a copy of Nadal's work had arrived in China. The first Jesuit to attempt to reproduce it in China was made by João da Rocha, S.J. (1565–1623). Father Rocha engaged the well-known scholar and painter Dong Qichang (1555–1636) or one of his students to adapt the illustrations from Nadal's work to China. Later, in 1635–1637, while working in Fuzhou, Aleni and three other Jesuits produced a Chinese version of Nadal's work consisting of fifty engravings and a cover page. It was entitled *The Incarnation of the Lord of Heaven through Illustrations and Commentary*. With considerable effort, the copper engravings of Nadal's work were transformed into Chinese wood carvings, with a delightful result (see figure 2.2).

Gradually the process of Sinicizing these European techniques moved forward. Whereas the characters in Cheng Dayue's collection had distinctly European features, the forty-eight pictures on biblical themes presented in 1640 by Father Schall to the last Ming ruler, the Chongzhen Emperor (r. 1628–1643), revealed Chinese features. Three of these pictures were reproduced in the notoriously anti-Christian work *I Cannot Do Otherwise* (ca. 1664) by Yang Guangxian described in the next chapter (see figure 2.3).

The Jesuits also used visual art to teach Catholic catechism. Some of this artwork was disseminated in inexpensive, popular form. However, examples of these works have become very rare, such that today they are often held in private collections. Recently, a remarkable example of this genre of artwork came to light through a published Sotheby's catalog (1988) of the

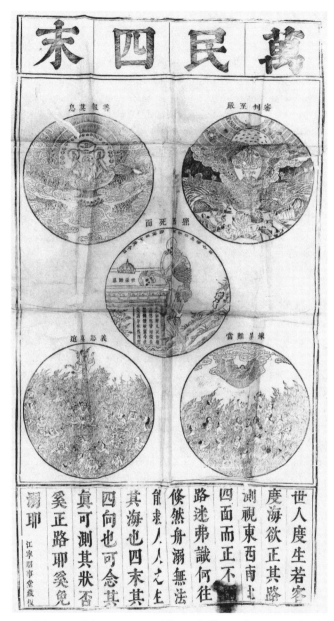

Figure 2.4. "Picture of the Four Last Things of All People" (*Wanmin simo tu*), ca. 1683, by Andrea-Giovanni Lubelli, S.J., with five tondi printed sheet, 143 by 24 inches, private collection. Permission of Maggs Bros. Ltd. The five tondi present Death (middle), Judgment (upper right), Heaven (upper left), Purgatory (lower right), and Hell (lower left). Purgatory is not one of the Four Last Things because it is a transitional state between death and Heaven and not final in nature. The Chinese features of the human figures indicate that the drawing was made by a Chinese artist under Father Lubelli's direction.

sale of items from an estate sale. This work, entitled "Picture of the Four Last Things of All People" (*Wanmin simo tu*), that is, Death, Judgment, Hell, and Heaven, is apparently one of several copies produced by Chinese woodblock printing created by the Jesuits to issue a stern warning on human fate. "Picture of the Four Last Things of All People" (*Wanmin simo tu*) is printed on an oversize sheet of paper (see figure 2.4) and consists of five tondi (circular drawings) with Chinese captions and text. The center tondo represents Death, while the other tondi represent (in clockwise order) Judgment (upper right), Purgatory (lower right), Hell (lower left), and Heaven (upper left). Since Purgatory is transitory rather than eternal, it is technically not one of the Four Last Things.

Although the imagery derives from European sources, they reveal how the assimilation of Christianity was occurring in China. The distinctly Chinese physical features of the people portrayed in these tondi indicate that they were drawn by Chinese artists under the direction of a European Jesuit. The drawings are quite vivid and meant to serve as a warning, causing people to meditate on their eventual fate. The work is attributed to Andrea-Giovanni Lubelli (1611–1685) whose Chinese writings consisted mainly of catechetical instructions and focused on teaching people to prepare for the life to come. It is likely that Lubelli had assistance from Chinese literati in writing the text in addition to the craftsmen who carved the woodblock. The Heaven (top left) and Judgment (top right) tondi are based on pictures in Nadal's work that was adapted by the Jesuit Giulio Aleni to produce a Chinese edition (cited above). The tondo featuring Death (center) is a slightly revised version of one of the skeletons in the famous book on anatomy *De humani corporis fabrica* (1543) by Andreas Vesalius. The tondi for Purgatory (lower left) and Hell (lower right) have not been traced to a European source. Certainly the Chinese artist would have been familiar with images of hell from Buddho-Daoist popular religion.

WORKS CONSULTED

Bailey, Gauvin Alexander. *Art on the Jesuit Missions in Asia and Latin America, 1542–1773*. Toronto: University of Toronto Press, 1999.

Chan, Albert. *Chinese Books and Documents in the Jesuit Archives in Rome: A Descriptive Catalogue. Japonica-Sinica 1–4*. Armonk, N.Y.: M. E. Sharpe, 2002.

Charbonnier, Jean-Pierre. *Christians in China: A.D. 600 to 2000*. Translated by M. N. L. Couve de Murville. San Francisco: Ignatius Press, 2007.

Chaves, Jonathan. "Moral Action in the Poetry of Wu Chia-chi (1618–84)." *Harvard Journal of Asiatic Studies* 46 (1986): 420–22.

Chesneaux, Jean. *Peasant Revolts in China, 1840–1949*. Translated by C. A. Curwen. New York: W. W. Norton, 1973.

Cippola, Carlo. *Clocks and Culture, 1300–1700*. New York: W. W. Norton, 1967.

Cohen, Paul A. *China and Christianity: The Missionary Movement and the Growth of Antiforeignism, 1860–1870*. Cambridge, Mass.: Harvard University Press, 1963.

Collani, Claudia von. "Charles Maigrot's Role in the Chinese Rites Controversy." In *The Rites Controversy: Its History and Meaning*, edited by D. E. Mungello, 149–83. Nettetal, Germany: Steyler Verlag, 1994.

Corsi, Elisabetta. *La Fábrica de las Ilusiones: Los Jesuitas y la Difusión de la Perspectiva Lineal en China, 1698–1766*. Mexico: El Colegio de México, Centro de Estudios de Asia y África, 2004.

De Angelis, Bernardo. "Carta a los Padres Provincials de Roma a 12 de octubre 1601." *Monumenta Mexicana* 7 (1599–1602), edited by Felix Zubillaga, 766–71. Rome: Institutum Historicum Societatis Iesu, 1981.

Dehergne, Joseph. *Répertoire des Jésuites de Chine de 1552 à 1800*. Rome: Institutum Historicum Societatis Iesu, 1973.

Dudink, Ad. "In Memoriam: Erik Zürcher (1928–2008)." *Sino-Western Cultural Relations Journal* 30 (2008): 1–16.

———. "Lubelli's *Wanmin simo tu* (Picture of the Four Last Things of All People), ca. 1683." *Sino-Western Cultural Relations Journal* 28 (2006): 1–17.

Dunne, George H. *Generation of Giants: The Story of the Jesuits in China in the Last Decades of the Ming Dynasty*. Notre Dame, Ind.: University of Notre Dame, 1962.

Elvin, Mark. *The Pattern of the Chinese Past: A Social and Economic Interpretation*. Stanford, Calif.: Stanford University Press, 1973.

Foss, Theodore N. "A Western Interpretation of China: Jesuit Cartography." In *East Meets West: The Jesuits in China, 1582–1773*, edited by Charles E. Ronan and Bonnie B. C. Oh, 209–51. Chicago: Loyola University Press, 1988.

Fu, Lo-shu. *A Documentary Chronicle of Sino-Western Relations (1644–1820)*. 2 vols. Tucson: University of Arizona Press, 1966.

Hudson, G. F. *Europe and China: A Survey of Their Relations from the Earliest Times to 1800*. London: Edward Arnold, 1931.

Hummel, Arthur W., ed. *Eminent Chinese of the Ch'ing Period (1644–1912)*. Washington, D.C.: U.S. Government Printing Office, 1943.

Jami, C., and H. Delahaye, eds. *L'Europe en Chine: Interactions scientifiques, religieuses et culturelles aux dix-septième et dix-huitième siècles*. Paris: De Boccard, 1993.

Kuhn, Philip A. *Soulstealers: The Chinese Sorcery Scare of 1768*. Cambridge, Mass.: Harvard University Press, 1990.

Lee, Archie C. C. "Cross-textual Reading Strategy: A Study of Late Ming and Early Qing Chinese Writings." *Ching Feng*, new series 1, no. 4 (2003): 1–27.

Li Jiubiao. *Kuoduo richao. Li Jiubiao's Diary of Oral Admonitions. A Late Ming Christian Journal.* Translated by Erik Zürcher. 2 vols. Nettetal, Germany: Steyler Verlag, 2007.

Mungello, D. E. *Drowning Girls in China: Female Infanticide Since 1650.* Lanham, Md.: Rowman & Littlefield, 2008.

———. *The Forgotten Christians of Hangzhou.* Honolulu: University of Hawaii Press, 1994.

Murray, John J. *Antwerp in the Age of Plantin and Brueghel.* Norman: University of Oklahoma Press, 1970.

Pagani, Catherine. *"Eastern Magnificence and European Ingenuity": Clocks of Late Imperial China.* Ann Arbor: University of Michigan Press, 2001.

Peterson, Willard J. "Why Did They Become Christians? Yang T'ing-yun, Li Chihtsao, and Hsü Kuang-ch'i." In *East Meets West: The Jesuits in China, 1582–1773,* edited by Charles E. Ronan and Bonnie B. C. Oh., 129–52. Chicago: Loyola University Press, 1988.

Pfister, Louis. *Notices biographiques et bibliographiques sur les Jésuites de l'ancienne Mission de Chine, 1552–1773.* Shanghai: Mission Catholique, 1932–1934.

Ricci, Matteo. *The True Meaning of the Lord of Heaven (T'ien-chu Shih-i).* Translated by Douglas Lancashire and Peter Hu Kuo-chen. Edited by Edward J. Malatesta. St. Louis: Institute of Jesuit Sources, 1985.

Rosso, Antonio Sisto, O.F.M. *Apostolic Legations to China of the Eighteenth Century.* Pasadena, Calif.: Perkins, 1948.

Sachsenmaier, Dominic. *Die Aufnahme europäischer Inhalte in die chinesische Kultur durch Zhu Zongyuan (ca. 1616–1660).* Nettetal, Germany: Steyler Verlag, 2001.

Sinica Franciscia. Vol. X, *Relationes et epistolas Fratrum Minorum Hispanorum in sinis qui annis 1696–98 missionem ingress sunt.* Compiled and edited by Antonius [Sixto] Rosso, O.F.M.; prepared for publication and corrected by Fathers Gaspar Han (Han Chengliang) and Antolin Abad, O.F.M. 2 parts. Madrid: Segretaria della Missioni, 1997.

Spence, Jonathan S. *The Memory Palace of Matteo Ricci.* New York: Viking, 1984.

Standaert, Nicolas. *The Fascinating God: A Challenge to Modern Chinese Theology Presented by a Text on the Name of God Written by a 17th Century Chinese Student of Theology.* Rome: Editrice Pontifica Università Gregoriana, 1995.

———. "Inculturation and Chinese-Christian Contacts in Late Ming and Early Qing." *Ching Feng* (Hong Kong) 34, no. 4 (December 1991): 1–16.

———. "New Trends in the Historiography of Christianity in China." *Catholic Historical Review* 83, no. 4 (October 1997): 573–613.

———. *Yang Tingyun: Confucian and Christian in Late Ming China.* Leiden, Netherlands: Brill, 1988.

Standaert, Nicolas, and Adrian Dudink, eds. *Chinese Christian Texts from the Roman Archives of the Society of Jesus.* 12 vols. Taipei, Taiwan: Ricci Institute, 2002.

Ter Haar, B. J. *The White Lotus Teachings in Chinese Religious History.* Leiden, Netherlands: Brill, 1992.

Tsien, Tsuen-hsuin. "Western Impact on China through Translation." *Far Eastern Quarterly* 18 (1954): 305–27.

Väth, Alfons. *Johann Schall von Bell, S.J. Missionar in China, kaiserlicher Astronom und Ratgeber am Hofe von Peking 1592–1666*, 1933; rev. ed. Nettetal, Germany: Steyler Verlag, 1991.

Verhaeren, H. *Catalogue de la bibliothèque du Pé-t'ang*. Beijing: Lazaristes, 1949.

———. "Ordonnances de la Sainte Eglise" (in French and Chinese). *Monumenta Serica* (Beiping) 4 (1939–1940): 451–77.

Wakeman, Frederic, Jr. *The Great Enterprise: The Manchu Reconstruction of Imperial Order in Seventeenth-Century China*. 2 vols. Berkeley and Los Angeles: University of California Press, 1985.

Waley-Cohen, Joanna. *The Sextants of Beijing: Global Currents in Chinese History*. New York: W. W. Norton, 1999.

Young, John D. *Confucianism and Christianity: The First Encounter*. Hong Kong: University of Hong Kong Press, 1983.

Zürcher, E. *Bouddhisme, Christianisme et société chinoise*. Paris: Julliard, 1990.

———. "Confucian and Christian Religiosity in Late Ming China." *Catholic Historical Review* 83, no. 4 (October 1997): 614–53.

3

CHINESE REJECTION
OF WESTERN CULTURE
AND CHRISTIANITY

THE BASIS OF ANTI-CHRISTIAN FEELING IN CHINA

Whereas the literati's interest in Christianity weakened (but never died) over the course of the seventeenth century, small numbers of lower-class Chinese continued to be converted by non-Jesuit missionaries, particularly the Franciscans and Dominicans. However, anti-Christian feeling grew in China as the seventeenth and eighteenth centuries progressed.

One basis of anti-Christian feeling in China was Confucian religious skepticism and agnosticism. There is an often quoted passage in the Confucian classic the *Analects* (chap. 11:12) in which Confucius speaks of avoiding spirits. It has never been fully clarified whether Confucius was simply showing respect for spiritual things or whether he was expressing an attitude of agnostic humanism, but where some have seen ambiguity, the Jesuits saw an opportunity for harmonizing Confucianism with Christianity. The Jesuits viewed the lack of religious emphasis in Confucianism as a basis for blending its moral and social strains with the explicitly religious strains of Christianity. Whereas Buddhism and popular Daoism were explicitly religious and fraught with heterodoxies in the eyes of Christians, Confucianism was only implicitly religious and so less explicitly heterodox. Still, there was a strain of religious skepticism in Confucianism that caused many literati to reject the mystical elements of Christianity (the Virgin Birth, the Incarnation, the miraculous healings, the Resurrection, and the Trinity).

A second basis of anti-Christian feeling among the literati was Chinese ethnocentrism, or the belief that Chinese culture was superior to other cultures. The Chinese literati believed in the Transmission of the Way (*Dao tong*) by which truth was handed down from the ancients to Confucius and, in turn, to other literati down to the present. Many literati believed that participation in the tradition was necessary for something to be true; they called this tradition "the true Way" (*zheng Dao*). The false way was referred to by various terms (*xie, yiduan,* and *zuodao*), all of which meant "false" and "heterodox" and carried connotations of being different in a way that is not Chinese.

The Chinese literati were not unique in developing such an ethno-centric view of truth. The Spanish missionaries who came out of a Reconquista atmosphere tended to see Christian truth in a similar way. Both the Chinese and Spanish views mixed a high degree of cultural factors into their view of religious truth. But just as the Spanish missionaries did not represent the views of all Christian missionaries in China, neither did the ethnocentric views of some literati represent the outlook of all Chinese literati. Literati who converted to Christianity, or who at least were sympathetic to its teachings, believed that the truths of the ancients were not limited to the Chinese because the ancients spoke primarily as human beings rather than as Chinese. (Europeans who were sympathetic to Chinese philosophy also tended to believe that the biblical patriarchs spoke primarily as human beings rather than as members of a Western race.) These literati tended to interpret certain passages from the classics to support their views.

For example, Shang Huqing, in a preface to *The Touchstone of True Knowledge* (*Zhengxiu liushi*) (1698), cited the Confucian classic *Mencius* (chap. IV.b) to make the point that the legendary sage-ruler Shun (2255–2205 BC) and King Wen (ca. 1050 BC), although originating in places over a thousand *li* (333 miles) apart and with a thousand years separating them, had identical standards as sages. Shang wrote that regardless of whether one's homeland is north, south, east, or west, the minds and principles of the sages are the same. In the last chapter, we noted how the Christian literatus Zhang Xingyao had claimed that "in the Eastern Sea and Western Sea sages arise who are identical in thinking." While Christians like Shang and Zhang constituted a very small percentage of the literati, views about the universality of sagehood were widely held among the literati.

From the outset, Christianity evoked hostile sentiments among the Chinese literati who saw it in much the same way that many of them saw Buddhism and Daoism. These teachings were viewed as false because they were heterodox; in fact, the terms "heterodoxy" and "falsehood" became synonymous. The term "Confucianism" is rarely used by the Chinese and is a Western construct, created by Europeans in the seventeenth century. The Chinese themselves call this philosophy the "Literati Teaching," and it represents a tradition of wisdom handed down from antiquity. Confucius himself said that he was simply transmitting the wisdom of antiquity and not creating it. In fact, to claim the truths associated with the Confucian tradition as a personal creation of Confucius would be to demean these truths as being the insights of only one man. While it is difficult to trace the truths to their precise ancient forms, it is very clear that the teachings associated with Confucius were further developed in later years by other literati, so that the Confucianism of the seventeenth century (Neo-Confucianism) was far more complex than the philosophy that Confucius himself had taught, although the philosophy certainly attempted to be true to the essential teachings of the master. The accusations of heterodoxy against Christianity were reinforced by members of secret societies who sought baptism solely to secure the limited protection Christianity had received in the toleration edicts extended by the imperial court.

The intellectual basis of anti-Christian attitudes in China was found largely in Neo-Confucian thinkers whose opposition to Christianity involved more than ethnocentrism. The intellectual grounds to this opposition derived from Neo-Confucian cosmology, a dimension of Confucian philosophy that had not yet been developed during Confucius's time. While Confucius himself may have avoided mentioning spirits and not discussed transcendent concerns, Neo-Confucian morality was based upon a cosmological ground that had explicit religious dimensions. For this reason, Matteo Ricci and other Jesuits criticized Neo-Confucianism and favored the "original Confucianism" of Confucius, which lacked these religious elements that conflicted with Christianity. The most basic element of Neo-Confucian cosmology was *Taiji* (the Supreme Ultimate), which generates the world in a way quite different from Christian Creation (see figure 3.1). According to Neo-Confucian cosmology formulated in the Song dynasty by Zhou Dunyi (1017–1073) and later incorporated into the Neo-Confucian philosophy of Zhu Xi (1130–1200), the universe consists of ongoing processes of generation and corruption, with different stages occurring simultaneously. The Diagram of the Supreme Ultimate reduces these processes to their simplest level, which begins with unity and then divides into active *yang* and quiescent *yin* forces; yang and yin then further divide into increasing diversity (the five elements, etc.), which eventually returns to unity, and the cycle repeats its course. Neo-Confucians did not see Heaven (*Tian*) as a supreme personal being like the Christians, and they were highly critical of Ricci's use of the Confucian classics to support Christianity.

Another source of anti-Christian feeling was based on the Chinese fear of subversion. This issue became more important after the Manchus came to power in 1644. The Manchus were military conquerors who constituted a tiny minority in the vast population of China. They lived in a perpetual

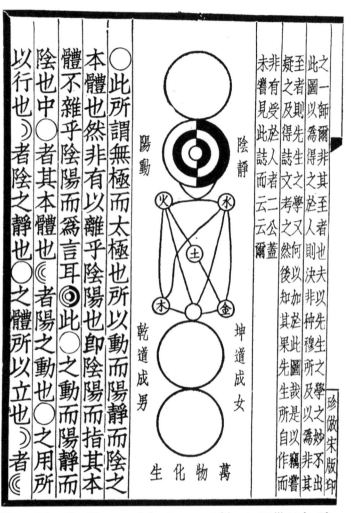

Figure 3.1. The Diagram of the Supreme Ultimate (*Taiji tu*) by Zhou Dunyi (1017–1073). The Supreme Ultimate was the cornerstone of Neo-Confucian cosmology. This illustration is from the *Xingli jingyi* (Essential Meaning of the School of Nature and Principle, i.e., Neo-Confucianism), compiled by Li Guangdi in 1715 by order of the Kangxi Emperor. The diagram represents the different stages of generation and corruption in the universe, with the identical circles at the top and bottom indicating the cyclical nature of this process. The second circle represents division into yang and yin forces, while the middle portion represents further differentiation into the five elements (earth, fire, water, wood, and metal). This cyclical nature conflicted with the Judeo-Christian notion of Creation *ex nihilo* (out of nothing) described in Genesis.

state of anxiety over threats to their control of the majority population. This concern caused them to pressure the scholar-officials to be constantly on the alert against subversive activity. The hypersensitivity of the Manchu throne to such activity was demonstrated in the Chinese sorcery scare of 1768, when it was believed that sorcerers were clipping queues (a Manchu-style pigtail, shown in figure 1.2, imposed on all Chinese males after the conquest of 1644). Beginning in the lower Yangzi River region near Suzhou, wandering Buddhist monks and other homeless people generated hysteria among the populace by spreading rumors that the sorcerers had the power to use the clipped queue in a form of black magic. The magic was aimed particularly at prized male children, who would become ill and possibly even die through the loss of part of their soul. Although the imperial authorities were skeptical of the claims of the sorcerers' powers, they were concerned that the clipping of queues (an illegal act) signified subversive activity, and Manchu paranoia over this issue exaggerated the danger.

It was the missionaries' foreign status and their association with the aggressive Portuguese and Dutch traders on the southeast coast of China that raised the fear of subversion. Although such a threat might appear ridiculous in light of the relative sizes of China and these European nations in the seventeenth century, the damage done to Chinese shipping and to the coastal villages in Fujian was considerable. Moreover, by the end of the eighteenth century, the balance of power was shifting, and beginning in 1839 with the Opium War (or First Anglo-Chinese War), smaller European nations began inflicting a series of humiliating military defeats upon the Chinese. There were isolated European proposals to invade China, but none were implemented. In short, the Manchu fear of subversion from the European missionaries, while greatly exaggerated, was not entirely unfounded.

Another basis for anti-Christian feeling was widespread concern among the Chinese populace that Christian churches might upset the harmony of nature. The Chinese had a very strong belief in geomancy, or *feng-shui* (literally, wind and water). Geomancy involves the belief that one's fortune can be enhanced by constructing buildings, homes, and graves in harmony with the physical surroundings. Conversely, one can suffer ill fortune if these sites are built in opposition to geomantic forces. The primary geomantic force is called the "cosmic breath" (*qi*). It consists of the celestial forces of yin and yang, whose outward signs are the physical forms of wind and water. The determination of a building or burial site involves the analysis of factors such as location, terrain, foundation, surroundings, streams flowing past the site, and direction or orientation. The aim is to determine the most harmonious placement of the building or grave in relationship to these forces, which, in turn, will produce the most favorable experience for the occupants of the building or the descendants of the deceased in the grave. The construction of Christian, particularly European-style, churches, and especially towers and crosses on the exterior, was sometimes believed to violate the harmony of the geomantic forces in the area and was thought to create an unfavorable atmosphere for those Chinese who lived and worked nearby.

Yet another basis of anti-Christian feeling directed toward the European priests was the fear that they would seduce Chinese women. This was particularly the case among more affluent families, in which the women were largely secluded within the home. In seventeenth- and eighteenth-century China, Christian churches were often built with separate chapels for women. If there was only one chapel that had to be shared, the women used it at a separate time; it was absolutely forbidden that men enter the chapel, or even look into it from the outside, when the women were using it. However, certain rites required close contact between the priest and women. In the administration of the sacraments, which involved touching the women, priests were sometimes accused of fondling the women's breasts. Accusations of improprieties in the act of confession were sometimes handled by having a mat hung between the priest and confessant with an observer at the other end of the room, close enough to see that nothing improper happened between the priest and the woman confessing, yet far enough away so that the words of the confession and the priest's response could not be heard.

Chinese fears of the sexual seduction of young women by European priests were exaggerated but not groundless. The number of known cases of such seduction is very small, but it is likely that some incidents have been suppressed by a powerful church and faithful communicants. Nevertheless, a few cases are known. One case involved two Propaganda missionaries working under the pressures of an underground church in 1738–1739 in remote areas of southern Zhili province, approximately two hundred miles south of Beijing.

Although the two missionaries were members of the same order and well acquainted, their cases were somewhat different. Bernardino Maria Bevilacqua, O.F.M., came from the remote Calabria region of the southern Italian peninsula. He was a member of the Franciscan order sent to China by Propaganda. Because the missionaries had been officially expelled from China in 1732, they were working secretly in their mission sites in Shandong and Zhili provinces. They lived in remote villages, in constant fear of being discovered and arrested. Bevilacqua appears to have cracked under the stress of such living conditions and began taking advantage of his priestly authority to seduce several young Catholic women.

Some of these young women were virgins (two of them were only twelve and fourteen years old) and others were recently married. The four-teen-year-old girl, apparently fearful of being unable to conceive, came to Father Bevilacqua asking for prayers in dealing with her irregular menstrual cycle. He convinced her that he could regularize her cycle and, in the process, violated her sexually. Afterward, when the young woman attempted to hang herself out of humiliation, her parents discovered the facts and sought help from Bevilacqua's superior, Father Giovanni Antonio Boucher. Boucher believed that Bevilacqua was crazed by a form of demonic posses-sion and had him removed from the mission field and sent to Macau im-mediately. In addition, Boucher paid silver to the injured families and was persuasive in attributing Bevilacqua's transgressions to satanic influences. Fi-nally, Boucher imposed a vow of silence on everyone involved.

Soon afterward, in 1739, a second Propaganda missionary, Allesio Ran-danini, O.F.M. (b. 1693), was accused of attempting to purchase the sexual services of a non-Christian woman. Boucher removed him from the mis-sion without delay. The scandal was able to remain buried for 250 years not only because Boucher acted promptly but also because he used a secret code in communicating details of this scandal to his superior in Rome. The most delicate details were described with a phonetic form of Chinese characters in which the pronunciation of the Chinese characters was given in the Latin alphabet. Such a code would have been decipherable only by someone who was fluent in the Mandarin (*guanhua*) dialect of northern China.

A seventh basis of anti-Christian feeling involved what the Chinese scholar Huang Yilong calls a "two-headed snake (*liang tou xia*)," a classical metaphor from the sixth century BC. This metaphor refers to the irresolv-able conflict experienced by the first generations of Chinese Christians in the late Ming and early Qing dynasties. This was the conflict between Christian monogamy and Confucian concubinage encountered by any bap-tized Chinese male. Christianity limited marriage to one wife. However, Confucian obligations for producing heirs (especially boys) to continue the ancestral line made polygamy a practical means for increasing one's chances of having children. This was a concern felt far more by affluent Chinese males, such as literati, than by poor Chinese males and may explain why Christianity made more conversions among poor country people than af-fluent gentry. Because of female infanticide and higher female mortality due to the malnourishment of girls, there was typically an imbalance in sex ra-tios in China with more males than females. Consequently, while literati were able to afford a wife and one or more concubines, many poor males remained unmarried.

A final basis of anti-Christian feeling was the belief that the missionaries practiced some form of alchemy. Daoist alchemy in China involved two very different goals, although in both cases chemical laboratories were used. One was an attempt to transmute base metals into silver (which was more highly valued in China than gold), and the other was an attempt to synthesize an elixir of immortality. The substance most commonly associated with this elixir was mercury in the form of its primary ore, cinnabar (red mercuric sulfide). When Ricci taught Christian immortality in China, many people confused Christian immortality with Daoist immortality.

This confusion was reinforced when Portuguese traders bought large quantities of mercury in Canton. It was shipped to Japan and India and to the Americas. This trade with the Americas led to one of the greatest early transfers of precious metals. The Spanish conquerors of the Inca empire discovered a large silver deposit in 1545 at Potosí located in the Andes Mountains thirteen thousand feet above sea level. The mining authorities discovered that a mercury refining process would increase the yields even though it devastated the miners with its poisonous effects. Beginning in the sixteenth century, Spanish ships crossed the Pacific Ocean carrying silver in the form of Mexican silver dollars. Massive amounts of New World silver entered China via Spanish ships at Manila and Portuguese ships at Macau. China's enormous economy and appetite for silver absorbed three-fourths of the New World silver during the years 1500–1800.

Since the Portuguese and Spanish boats on which this mercury was shipped out of China returned carrying silver, many Chinese concluded that the Europeans and missionaries were practicing alchemy. Ricci found these suspicions frustrating, particularly since Daoist immortality was physical and aimed at prolonging the life of the body whereas Christian immortality was spiritual and focused on the soul. He was constantly dealing with Chinese who were attracted to him for the wrong reason, namely, his supposed alchemical expertise rather than his spiritual teaching.

Unwittingly, the missionaries contributed to linking Christian teaching with the Daoist cultivation of physical immortality when they praised the delayed decomposition of a corpse as a sign of great spirituality. The Jesuit annual letter of 1678–1679 gives a detailed description of the intact nature of Father Martino Martini's body eighteen years after his death, speaking of the remarkably lifelike condition of Martini's hair, beard, and fingernails and of the absence of any unpleasant odor. Accounts of later vis-

Figure 3.2. The memorial gateway (*paifang*) and tomb of Martino Martini and twenty other Jesuits, built 1676–1678, Dafangjing Cemetery, outside Hangzhou. Annual visits until 1843 to the tomb by Hangzhou Christians to trim Martini's hair and nails confirmed the remarkable lack of corruption of Martini's body. While Christians interpreted this as a sign of great spirituality, Daoists saw it as a sign that Martini had practiced the art of alchemy.

its to Martini's gravesite in Hangzhou (see figure 3.2), one as late as 1843, continued to emphasize the lifelike appearance of Martini's corpse.

CHINESE ANTI-CHRISTIAN MOVEMENTS

Anti-Christian sentiments among the literati occasionally broke out into anti-Christian movements that occurred periodically throughout the seventeenth century. The first anti-Christian movement was centered in Nanjing in the years 1616–1621. It was instigated by the scholar-official Shen Que, who sought to uncover a subversive movement out of animosity toward Christians and to advance his own political career. In his petitions to the throne, Shen accused the foreign priests of misleading the people into following a criminal (Jesus) who was sentenced to death. He accused the missionaries of teaching the people to neglect their ancestors, offering money for conversions, and practicing rites that involved mixed sexes in debauchery. Shen accused the missionaries of cultivating high officials and gaining access to official documents. He claimed that they maintained contacts with the Portuguese at Macau, who were dangerous foreigners. He voiced suspicion about the missionaries' mysterious sources of funding.

Shen accused the missionaries of holding weekly secret meetings, controlling the people through magical arts, and keeping records of the names of their fellow conspirators. He noted similarities between these Christians and the outlawed White Lotus sect. (Christian converts on a higher social level were accused of constituting a literati faction.) The priests at Nanjing were arrested, and their residence was searched and an inventory made of the contents, but no weapons were found. Four Jesuits were expelled to Macau, but the expulsion was of short duration. The persecution was largely limited to Nanjing, and no one was put to death because of it. In the aftermath of the Nanjing persecution, the first anti-Christian Chinese work, *A Collection of Works Attacking Heterodoxy (Poxieji)*, appeared in 1639.

Far more destructive was the anti-Christian movement led from Beijing by the scholar-official Yang Guangxian beginning in 1664. Like Shen, Yang had an intense dislike of Christians, though his motives appear to have been more sincere and less for personal advancement. In fact, Yang appears to have been a dedicated Neo-Confucian who genuinely believed that Christianity was intellectually false and harmful to China. The intensity of Yang's beliefs led him to conduct a harsh attack against Father Johann Adam Schall von Bell that led to the execution of several of Schall's assistants. Yang accused Schall of causing the death of the Xiaoxian Empress and—because of the Shunzhi Emperor's grief over the loss of his favorite concubine—the premature death of the emperor himself. The basis of the accusation was that as head of the Bureau of Astronomy, Schall had brought the empress's death about by the selection of an inauspicious day for the burial of an imperial prince born to the Xiaoxian Empress and the Shunzhi Emperor. In the intense political atmosphere of the court, this charge gained credibility among the shamanistically-minded Manchus and an investigation was begun.

In the course of the investigation in early 1665, Schall—now an elderly seventy-two years old—suffered a stroke and became paralyzed. He had to be carried into the legal proceedings on a stretcher and had lost the ability to speak. He was assisted by Father Ferdinand Verbiest. Schall was found guilty and, along with the seven Chinese astronomers who assisted him, was sentenced to a lingering death. Later, five more Chinese were sentenced to death and the three Jesuits besides Schall then in Beijing were sentenced to flogging and exile. The day after the Judgment, an earthquake struck Beijing and a fire occurred in the palace. These were interpreted as acts of God that indicated Heaven's displeasure over the verdicts. All the accused were freed, except for five Chinese Christian astronomers, who served as scapegoats. They were blamed for choosing the inauspicious day of the prince's burial and were executed. The four Jesuits in Beijing were allowed to remain there, but all other missionaries were expelled to Macau until 1671, and the Christian churches in China were closed.

Yang was appointed in Schall's place to head the Bureau of Astronomy, but he was incompetent and unable to produce an accurate calendar. Father Verbiest challenged Yang and his associates to a competition involving an astronomical computation. When Western methods proved more accurate in several trials, Yang was removed as head of the bureau and replaced by Verbiest. Schall died on 15 August 1666, and soon thereafter the Kangxi Emperor ordered a review of the case. The verdicts against Schall and the executed Chinese astronomers were posthumously reversed, while Yang was disgraced and sentenced to death. In light of Yang's advanced age, his sentence was commuted to exile and he was allowed to return to his native home. Sick and weary, he died during the journey, but even from the grave Yang's spirit did not give up: A rumor circulated that the missionaries had poisoned him.

Yang wrote a caustically anti-Christian polemic entitled *I Cannot Do Otherwise* (*Budeyi*) in which he included illustrations of the Crucifixion (see figure 2.3). Yang argued that these pictures confirmed that Jesus was a subversive rebel leader (not unlike subversive rebels in China) who was convicted and executed for his crimes. For the Confucian literati, who were the guardians of law and order in China, such criticism was especially damning, and it found strong support among the literati. Although the Kangxi Emperor issued an edict of toleration of Christianity in 1692, his son, the Yongzheng Emperor, issued a countervailing edict in 1724 declaring Christianity a heterodox sect and closing the churches. Most of the missionaries were expelled, first to Canton and then to Macau, from 1724 to 1736. During this time, an underground church emerged in China with a number of missionaries secretly visiting their flocks, instructing neophytes, and baptizing converts. Christianity continued to suffer severe restrictions under the long reign of the Qianlong Emperor (r. 1736–1795).

Although the facts of history do not change, our understanding of them can develop and yield new insights. Thirty years ago, most scholars thought that the seventeenth-century Christian missionaries had failed to establish a lasting church in China. Today that view has been reversed. This lasting church was a minority church, but it continues in China today. The evolution of this interpretation is revealed in the work of two eminent Europeans. In 1982 the French Sinologist Jacques Gernet published a widely read book in which he argued that Christianity was unable to be assimilated in China because of fundamental cultural differences between China and Europe. According to Gernet, irreconcilable differences in the ways Chinese and Europeans thought were produced by differences in the Chinese and Indo-European languages. He claimed that Greek philosophy and medieval Scholastic philosophy could not have been developed had they been based upon the Chinese language because the latter lacks the verb "to be" and the concept of "being." He argued that there was no Chinese word to denote the concept of being or essence. The Chinese were not philosophically unsophisticated, and Gernet claims that they were the only civilization not based on the Indo-European languages to develop complete philosophical thought. Whereas the Indo-European languages were well suited to fostering the Christian elements of transcendental and immutable realities, the Chinese language was more inclined to see realities in terms of the senses, which are transitory. Gernet's interpretation has been much disputed, but one should note that he uses it to explain that the Chinese reaction to Christianity was not merely xenophobic (a hatred of things foreign) but rather was based upon cultural differences. Gernet's work, like Joseph R. Levenson's work cited in chapter 1, was brilliant, but time has shown it to be wrong.

Unlike Gernet, the late Dutch Sinologist Erik Zürcher evolved in his thinking on this important question. In 1988, when he was invited by Gernet to give a lecture at Paris, Zürcher largely agreed with Gernet's interpretation, though he offered a different explanation for the failure of Christianity to be assimilated into seventeenth- and eighteenth-century China. Drawing from his earlier study of the assimilation of Buddhism into China early in the first millennium, Zürcher argued that Christianity was rejected because of the overly centralized direction of the Jesuits by a Counter-Reformation church and because of the incompatibility in China of the Jesuit dual roles of scholar and priest. However Zürcher's later study of Chinese Christian texts caused him to modify his point of view, at least to the extent of admitting that there had been a regional acceptance of Christianity by lower-ranking literati in Fujian province, as revealed in the diary of the Christian literatus Li Jiubiao.

In fact, the Chinese rejection of Christianity was neither total nor permanent. Christianity continued to ebb and flow in its development in China. In Japan in the years 1549–1614, the response to missionaries was initially far more enthusiastic than in China, producing perhaps three hundred thousand Christians out of a population of approximately twenty million. However, the government's persecution of Christians reduced them to an underground church that never recovered its previous vitality. In China, by contrast, the number of Christians declined from approximately three hundred thousand to two hundred thousand during the eighteenth century, but Christianity survived, particularly in more remote areas, such as Sichuan province. The regional history of rural villages in western Shandong and southern Zhili provinces shows that Christianity was absorbed into the family structure as whole families followed the family head in being baptized. In subsequent generations, Chinese filial piety caused their descendants to remain loyal to the Christianity of their ancestors. This phenomenon appears to have been repeated throughout China and explains the remarkable survival of Christianity in China down to the present.

Since the late 1500s, Christianity has continued to ebb and flow in its development in China, although sometimes it has given the appearance of being exterminated. As recently as the early 1970s, many China scholars believed that Christianity had been largely eradicated in China, but later events proved that the religion had merely been driven underground by persecution. It could be argued that seeds sown by Christian missionaries in the sixteenth through eighteenth centuries simply took several centuries to harvest. Such a long-term perspective is particularly appropriate for a nation with a history as long as China's.

EUROPEAN ART AT THE CHINESE COURT

The encounter between European and Chinese visual arts occurred in two different areas: within the imperial court and outside of the court in the churches and among the literati. Whereas the demands of the court tended to produce imitation of European paintings by Chinese craftsmen-artists, the encounter among the literati stimulated some creative responses among literati-artists. However, the Western influence upon Chinese artists was not widespread and was limited to a small number of literati-artists.

Although Ricci had established the first Jesuit residence in Beijing in 1601, it was not until after the Manchu conquest of China in 1644 that European painters worked at the imperial court. The first of these mostly Jesuit European painters appears to have been Johann Grueber, S.J. (1623–1680), of Austria. Perhaps the greatest Manchu ruler was the Kangxi Emperor (r. 1661–1722), and the first European painter at his court was the Jesuit lay brother Cristoforo Fiori, a twenty-four-year-old Italian who arrived at the court in 1694. Nothing is known of his artistic work, and after finding religious life too demanding, Fiori left the Jesuit order in 1705.

In addition to Giovanni Gherardini, Father Joachim Bouvet also brought the Jesuit lay brother Charles de Belleville (1657–1730) from France to Beijing in 1699. Belleville was an artist of diverse talents, including sculpture, painting of miniature portraits, and architecture. His artwork completed the Beitang Church in 1703, and he taught painting to young eunuchs at the court. Unable to tolerate the harsh climate of Beijing, he returned to Europe in 1707.

The next artist to arrive was Matteo Ripa (1682–1746) of Naples. Ripa was not associated with the Jesuits. He had been trained and sent out by Propaganda and was affiliated with the ill-fated embassy of the papal legate Thomas Maillard de Tournon, who was an opponent of the Jesuits. Nevertheless, the Kangxi Emperor valued artistic talent so highly that he did not allow his negative feelings toward Cardinal Tournon to deny him the services of a capable artist. The emperor, obsessed with the loss of Gherardini, asked "a thousand times" (according to Ripa) if he knew how to paint in perspective. Ripa consistently replied that he was not trained in perspective, but rather in portrait painting.

In 1712 the emperor asked Father Ripa to draw thirty-six views of his summer mountain retreat near Rehe (Jehol) in Manchuria and then etch them on copper. Ripa tried to decline the assignment on the grounds that he was a portrait painter rather than a landscape artist and that moreover he had no experience in making copper engravings. However, the emperor insisted, and Ripa completed the assignment in 1714, producing the first copper engravings in China, where wood engravings had traditionally been used. That same year the Kangxi Emperor ordered Ripa to make copper engravings of the Jesuit map of China, Manchuria, and Korea. This was done in forty-four plates.

The most famous Jesuit artist in China was Giuseppe Castiglione (b. 1688) of Milan. Because of the difficulty in retaining artists in Beijing, the Jesuits sought to find a dedicated member of their order who also a skilled artist. This individual was found in the lay brother Castiglione, a prolific artist whose canvases painted in churches in Genoa and Coimbra (Portugal) are still extant. He arrived in Beijing in December 1715. Almost immediately the Kangxi Emperor tried to induce him and Father Ripa to paint in enamels, but they both resisted until released from the assignment. (Later, in 1719, a trained enameller arrived in Beijing in the person of the Jesuit lay brother Jean-Baptist Gravereau, who unfortunately was forced to return to France in 1722 because of illness.)

Castiglione served three emperors (Kangxi, Yongzheng, and Qianlong) for fifty-one years, until his death in 1766. In addition to producing numerous paintings, he helped to design the Summer Palace (Yuanmingyuan) in the western suburbs of Beijing. Although Castiglione was trained in oil painting, the dominant medium of European painters since the sixteenth century, oil painting was not an object of great enthusiasm among the Chinese. On one notable occasion, the Qianlong Emperor complained about the hasty darkening of some poorly mixed oil paints. Nevertheless, the court utilized the missionary artists' realistic skills in portrait painting. Members of the royal family and court officials enthusiastically sat for portraits, and the Qianlong Emperor himself sat for three painters (Castiglione; Ignaz Sichelbarth, S.J. [1708–1780], of Bohemia; and Giuseppi Panzi of Paris).

From both an artistic and a missionary point of view, Jesuit painters at the palace in Beijing faced many restrictions. They were forced to serve long hours in the imperial workshop, working alongside Chinese court painters and craftsmen who had a low status in the palace. The atmosphere was competitive and sometimes hostile. Both the content and the style of their artistic work were determined by imperial commands. Jean-Denis Attiret, S.J. (1702–1768), who had come to decorate Jesuit churches, ended up painting endless portraits of members of the imperial family. Nevertheless, the missionary artists Castiglione, Sichelbarth, and Attiret were honored with high official rank by the Qianlong Emperor. Oftentimes they worked in collaboration with Chinese artists, for example, in portraits in which the European artists painted the faces while the Chinese artists did the costumes and backgrounds. This produced an eclectic Sino-European style in which Western influence in court painting reached its peak. The genre of imperial portraits and, to a lesser extent, landscape and architecture demonstrate this influence by which the use of perspective, chiaroscuro, and realism all appear. Sino-European style began under the Kangxi Emperor with the court painters Jiao Bingzhen and his pupil Leng Mei and peaked under the Qianlong Emperor, after which it went into decline.

Chinese artists known to have studied European painting and perspective under these missionaries included Ding Guanpeng, Zou Yigui, Shen Quan, and Xu Yang, in addition to the previously mentioned Yu Wenhui (Manuel Pereira), Ni Yicheng (Jacques Niva), Jiao Bingzhen, and Leng Mei. Ironically, the well-known painter and poet Wu Li (Wu Yushan) (1632–1718) was ordained as a Jesuit priest but exhibited no apparent Western influence in his paintings.

One of the most fascinating court paintings attributed to a missionary painter is the Fragrant Concubine (Xiang Fei) in European armor (see figure

3.3). The Fragrant Concubine is a figure who blends history with legend in a way that has yet to be unraveled. She is said to have been a Uighur. The Uighurs are a Muslim ethnic group concentrated in the northwestern Chinese province of Xinjiang ("New Territories"), an area that reaches into Central Asia and that was not incorporated into Qing China until the eighteenth century. According to legend, after the glorious defeat of the Uighurs in Altishahr (southern Xinjiang) in 1759, the triumphant Manchu general Zhaohui returned to Beijing with war booty, including the remarkable consort (other legends say daughter) of the Uighur leader Khozi Khan (Khoja Jihan). This strikingly beautiful woman was said to emit a natural fragrance and became known as the Fragrant Concubine.

Although given to the Qianlong Emperor as a concubine, she resisted any intimate contact with him and carried small knives in the sleeves of her clothing in order to avenge the loss of her homeland and her husband (or father), who was killed in the struggle. But the emperor was so entranced with her that he is said to have built a Muslim mosque and bazaar just beyond the southwest corner of the Beijing palace, near the South Sea. He also built a tower just inside the walls from which she could supposedly ease her homesickness by watching her fellow Muslims conducting business and going to the mosque. He is also said to have built a Turkish bathhouse called the Yudetang where the Fragrant Concubine could take steam baths to nurture her famously soft skin. The emperor, who had a close relationship with the painter Castiglione, is said to have ordered that he paint her portrait, with the result being the picture of the woman in armor.

The emperor's mother, the dowager empress, reportedly disliked her son's obsession with this woman, and one day when the emperor left the palace to perform the annual winter solstice sacrifices at the Altar of Heaven, she pounced. According to legend, she scolded the Fragrant Concubine for her behavior and said that she should either submit or die. One legend says that the Fragrant Concubine hanged herself while another says that she was strangled with a white silk scarf by two eunuchs. The emperor rushed back to the palace to save his concubine, but he was too late.

The problem with this drama is that much of it has no historical basis. There was a Uighur woman from Altishahr called Rong Fei who entered the imperial harem in 1760. She is presented in the historical records as a political symbol for the incorporation of Xinjiang into the Qing empire. However, she was not a close relative of the Uighur leaders, and there is little evidence that she played the role of a femme fatale or that the Qianlong Emperor was particularly obsessed with her. On the contrary, she had sex with him and gave birth to an imperial princess. She outlived the dowager

Figure 3.3.   Presumably a portrait of the Fragrant Concubine (Xiang Fei), concubine of the Qianlong Emperor, oil, attributed to G. Castiglione, circa 1760. Permission of the National Palace Museum, Taipei, Republic of China. The painting reflects the use of masquerade, a technique favored in Qing court portraits for political purposes. The portrait can possibly be traced to the historical Uighur concubine Rong Fei, who was brought to the court in 1760 and was later transformed by early twentieth-century revolutionary and feminist forces into the mythical Fragrant Concubine.

by several years and died a natural death in 1788. Her tomb has been located and was excavated in 1979. Her transformation into the legendary Fragrant Concubine occurred from the 1890s to 1950s as part of a series of politically revolutionary and feminist movements.

The portrait of the woman in armor was shown in the Yudetang bathhouse in 1914 and probably was painted by a missionary artist, possibly Castiglione. It was typical to have more than one version of court portraits made, and this may explain the existence of other versions of this portrait. European portraits were circulated in China by the early eighteenth century, and the Yongzheng Emperor had himself painted in European dress. The Yongzheng and Qianlong emperors used the medium of costume portraits of themselves as a political tool to convey their different roles (Confucian literatus, Buddhist bodhisattva, Daoist sage, Manchu hunter, etc.) and their affinities to different nationalities (Manchu, Han Chinese, Mongolian, Tibetan, etc.). The portrait of the Fragrant Concubine in Western armor presents a masquerade of a strutting male pose characteristic of numerous portraits of European monarchs. This probably reflects the European origins of the painter. However, why this military pose should be applied to the Fragrant Concubine (if it is the Fragrant Concubine) is a question that art historians have yet to answer.

EUROPEAN ART AMONG THE CHINESE LITERATI-PAINTERS

Because of the lack of literary documentation, it is difficult (and even controversial) to identify the Chinese professional and literati gentlemen painters who were influenced by European art. Nevertheless, by comparing their artworks to European works of art then circulating in China, several such artists have been identified. Most of them lived in the region of the lower Yangzi River and had access to Nanjing, an active missionary center believed to be the primary channel through which European artistic influence was spread to these Chinese artists.

The portraits of Zeng Jing (1568–1650) demonstrate a clear Western influence. Zeng was a native of the coastal province of Fujian, where there was considerable contact with missionaries and Portuguese traders. Later he moved to Nanjing, where Ricci was active around 1600 and where Zeng could have been exposed to European paintings and prints. Zeng incorporated Western realism into his portraits by applying many layers of color washes to a light ink outline. The effect produced features on the faces of his portraits that were akin to chiaroscuro. Using this technique, Zeng was able to paint portraits that reflect individualized qualities of personality and character. The creative power of Zeng's portraits was such that he had many followers among the Bochen school of professional portrait painters. Much debate has surrounded the claim that the famous Ming scholar–official painter Dong Qichang (1555–1636) produced an album of six paintings under the influence of an engraving by Antonius Wierix. These paintings, found today in the Museum of Natural History in New York, are signed with Dong's brush name, Xuan Cai, but the name may have been forged by an art dealer.

The influence of European art upon Chinese painting has until recently been regarded as minimal. Chinese landscape painting has been held in very high regard as a unique art form that differed from European painting both in technical medium (ink rather than oil) and content (stylized and abstract images of nature rather than realistic images and individualized portraits). In addition, the lack of documentation of contacts between Chinese artists and European art has been taken as confirmation of an absence of influence.

The art historian Michael Sullivan has argued that there were two main reasons for the lack of influence of European art on Chinese art. First, the number of Chinese artists who came into contact with European art was very small, and consequently the band of contact was very narrow. The two main points of contact were among the Nanjing school of painters in the seventeenth century and at the Beijing court throughout the eighteenth century. As the eighteenth century progressed, the Manchu throne grew increasingly defensive in mentality and reduced its contacts with Chinese literati and literati-painters, thereby further reducing the contacts between the European artists at court and the Chinese literati. By 1775 the former missionaries reported that the Qianlong Emperor had lost interest in his earlier plan of having European artists teach their skills to Chinese painters.

The second reason for the lack of Western influence on Chinese artists is that, in traditional China, it was the literati and not the court who established artistic standards. Most Chinese literati who had come into contact with Western art believed that its techniques of perspective and chiaroscuro were impressive but in the manner of artisans (craftsmen) rather than artists. Although Western painting would be more appreciated by the emerging merchant classes in the coastal areas of China during the late eighteenth and early nineteenth centuries, the literati remained the cultural arbiters of Chinese artistic taste until the late nineteenth century.

James Cahill has argued, contrary to the view of most art historians, that paintings by certain Chinese artists of the seventeenth and eighteenth

Figure 3.4.   View of Urbs Campensis, an anonymous engraving from *Civitatis Orbis Terrarum*, by Georg Braun and Franz Hogenberg, vol. 4 (Cologne, 1572–1616). Permission of the Herzog August Bibliothek Wolfenbüttel: 7.2 Hist 2?. By 1608 this volume had been carried to China, where it circulated among Chinese artists who were in contact with the missionaries.

centuries do reveal a European influence. Although the eighteenth-century influence, known through the paintings of Castiglione, is better known, its effect upon Chinese painters was slight. Cahill believes that the earlier seventeenth-century influence was far more creative and important in the history of Chinese painting. To support this view, he compares some late Ming paintings with late sixteenth-century German engravings of towns and cities (see figures 3.4 and 3.5). The European cityscapes (picture-maps) are drawn from a famous six-volume work published in Cologne in the years 1572–1616 entitled *Civitatis Orbis Terrarum*, by Georg Braun and Franz Hogenberg. The first volume had reached China by 1608, and the other volumes followed shortly thereafter.

One of the most striking examples of possible influence is taken from the album *Ten Scenes of Yue*, painted by Zhang Hong (1577–after 1652) from a journey he made to the historical region of Yue in eastern Zhejiang province in 1639. In one of these scenes, Zhang modified the traditional Chinese landscape. Instead of the traditional division into foreground and distant background separated by water, clouds, or fog, Zhang presents the

Figure 3.5.   Leaf from the album *Ten Scenes of Yue*, dated 1639 by Zhang Hong (1577–after 1652), ink on silk. Permission of the Museum Yamato Bunkakan, Nara, Japan. According to the art historian James Cahill, the joining of the upper and lower shores with this diagonal bridge was unprecedented in Chinese paintings and was influenced by the Chinese artist's exposure to European cityscapes, quite possibly the view of Urbs Campensis in figure 3.4.

near and far sides of a river connected by a diagonal bridge that narrows as it recedes into the distance (see figure 3.5). This scene is so unique in Chinese painting that Cahill feels that the view of Urbs Campensis in Braun and Hogenberg (figure 3.4) may have served as Zhang's model.

The striking parallels found in these comparisons are caused, according to Cahill, not by conscious imitation of European pictures on the part of the Chinese artist, but rather by some more indirect influence. If the Chinese artists had copied or imitated the European pictures, Cahill contends, the influence would be clearer but more superficial. Rather, he argues, the Chinese artists' exposure to European pictures was a powerful stimulus to their creativity; he believes the signs of that influence are found in the most original paintings in China at that time. In such powerfully creative artists, conscious imitation of European pictures was unlikely, but once such an artist saw the European works and absorbed them into his visual memory, then he (consciously or unconsciously) was influenced by the European models. The result was that European art was used creatively by a small number of Chinese artists to expand the traditional limits of their imaginative experience.

The painters whom Cahill and Sullivan identify as influenced by European techniques include Zhang Hong of Suzhou; Wu Bin (active ca. 1568–1625) of Fujian province and later Nanjing; Shen Shiqong (active ca. 1611–1640) of Songjiang; Shao Mi (active 1620–1660) of Suzhou; Zhao Zuo (active ca. 1610–1630), who was a close friend of the leading artist, Dong Qichang (1555–1636); Cui Zizhong (active 1600–1644); Gong Xian (ca. 1640–1689); the greatest of Nanjing painters, Li Yin (active ca. 1700) of Yangzhou; and Xiang Shengmo (1597–1658). Apart from landscapes, Sullivan claims that direct borrowing from Western sources is seen in the study of flowers and butterflies by Chen Hongshou (1598–1652). In summary, we can say that the influence of European art upon Chinese artists was limited but significant.

Most early Christian churches in China were built in the Chinese style, but because the Jesuit missionaries wished to distinguish their churches from Buddhist temples, a few churches were built in the baroque style, modeled after that most famous of baroque churches, Rome's Il Gesù. The cornerstone of St. Paul's (originally Mother of God) Church in Macau was laid in 1602. Although a fire in 1835 destroyed most of the church, the facade with statuary has survived as a commanding structure at the top of a broad stairway of 130 steps (see figure 3.6). Both the architect and its exact European model are unknown.

In Beijing, shortly before Ricci died in 1610, he initiated the construction of a church modeled after Il Gesù in Rome and St. Paul's in

Figure 3.6.   The facade of the Church of St. Paul in Macau, whose cornerstone
was laid in 1602. Courtesy of the Macau Government Tourist Office. The
church was designed by European Jesuits and built with the assistance of Japanese Christian craftsmen who had fled religious persecution in Nagasaki. The
church burned in 1835, leaving only the facade and the staircase.

Macau. The church was to be built in European style as an architectural witness to Christianity. Ricci collected fifty silver taels from the Christian scholar-official Li Zhizao and another donor. After Ricci's death, the church was constructed by Father Sabatino de Ursis, S.J. The church was built in the central part of Beijing near the Xuanwu Gate on land where the Jesuit residence was located. The church is described by an eyewitness account of 1635 as narrow and long (approximately forty-five feet by twenty-four feet) with a canopy-like ceiling, elaborate windows, and fine paintings done in Western style. Over the altar stood a painting of Jesus, whose lifelike appearance Chinese painting was said to have been unable to match. To the right of the hall was a chapel (probably for women) of the Virgin Mary, who was painted as a young girl holding the child Jesus. One of the most beautiful churches in China was a baroque-style church built in 1659–1663 in Hangzhou at the initiative of Father Martino Martini. This church was modeled very clearly on the Il Gesù in Rome and has survived to the present day, though the many devotional paintings that originally filled the church were destroyed by fire in 1692.

Music also played a role in the missionaries' plan for converting the Chinese. Two keyboard instruments, the clavichord and the harpsichord, became favored instruments at the imperial court. Both are stringed instruments, but in the clavichord the strings are struck by small hammers whereas in the harpsichord they are plucked. Ricci presented a clavichord to the Wanli Emperor in 1601 as a gift. These keyboard instruments fascinated the Chinese in part because they were mechanical devices akin to mechanical clocks and calendrical science but also because of their novel music-making qualities. Ricci arranged for the Jesuit Diego Pantoja to give daily lessons on the clavichord to four court eunuchs. This clavichord was preserved and rediscovered in 1640 when the last Ming emperor charged Father Schall to restore it.

Under the Kangxi Emperor, the Jesuit directors of the Chinese Bureau of Astronomy were also charged with being the imperial music teachers. Schall's successor, Ferdinand Verbiest, arranged for Father Tomé Pereira to be appointed palace musician and to play the harpsichord. The Kangxi Emperor himself even played a Chinese song on the harpsichord using one finger to pound out the melody. However, sometimes there were disasters, as in 1699 when a musical recital by five priests playing harpsichord, bassoon, bass viol, violin, and flute became so cacophonous to the Kangxi Emperor's ears that he abruptly stopped the recital.

The influence of the harpsichord at the Chinese court peaked with the arrival of the Lazarist Father Theodorico Pedrini in 1711. Pedrini knew not only how to play musical instruments but also how to build them. At the

Kangxi Emperor's request, he frequently played the harpsichord for the emperor and also tutored the emperor's sons in playing the Western keyboard. In addition, Pedrini composed twelve sonatas for violin and continuo of opus 3, whose manuscript was recently discovered in the Beijing National Library. The last of the missionary harpsichordists to play at the court was the Jesuit Father Joseph-Marie Amiot, who spent forty-three years at court, dying in 1793. However, the Qianlong Emperor had lost interest in European music long before Amiot's death.

In conclusion, although there was a broad-based rejection of Western culture and Christianity in seventeenth- and eighteenth-century China, the rejection was not total. Elements from Western religion and painting entered Chinese culture, and some of these elements would serve as seeds that, in the case of Christianity, would take many years to bear fruit.

WORKS CONSULTED

Arlington, L. C., and William Lewisohn. *In Search of Old Peking*. Beijing: Henri Vetch, 1935.

Barnard, Henri. "L'art chrétien en Chine du temps du P. Matthieu Ricci." *Revue d'histoire des missions* (Paris) 12 (1935): 199–229.

Brooks, E. Bruce, and A. Taeko Brooks. *The Original Analects: Sayings of Confucius and His Successors*. New York: Columbia, 1998.

Cahill, James. *The Compelling Image: Nature and Style in Seventeenth-Century Chinese Painting*. Cambridge, Mass.: Harvard University Press, 1982.

———. "Wu Pin and His Landscape Paintings." In *Proceedings of the International Symposium on Chinese Painting*, 637–98 plus 34 plates. Taipei, Taiwan: National Palace Museum, 1972.

Cameron, Nigel. *Barbarians and Mandarins: Thirteen Centuries of Western Travellers in China*. London: John Weatherhill, 1970.

Chan, Wing-tsit. "The *Hsing-li ching-i* and the Ch'eng-Chu School of the Seventeenth Century." In *The Unfolding of Neo-Confucianism*, edited by William Theodore de Bary, 543–79. New York: Columbia, 1975.

Chaves, Jonathan. *Singing of the Source: Nature and God in the Poetry of the Chinese Painter Wu Li*. Honolulu: University of Hawaii Press, 1993.

Ch'en Yuan. "Wu Yü-shan. In Commemoration of the 250th Anniversary of His Ordination to the Priesthood in the Society of Jesus." Adapted to English by Eugene Feifel. *Monumenta Serica* 3 (1937–1938): 130–70b.

Cohen, Paul A. *China and Christianity*. Cambridge, Mass.: Harvard University Press, 1963.

Corsi, Elisabetta. "Late Baroque Painting in China prior to the Arrival of Matteo Ripa: Giovanni Gherardini and the Perspective Painting Called *Xianfa*." In *Matteo*

Ripa e il Collegio dei Cinesi: La Missione cattolica in Cina tra i secoli XVIII–XIX, edited by Michele Fatica and Francesco D'Arelli, 103–22 plus 11 plates. Naples: Instituto Universitario Orientale, 1999.

De Groot, J. J. M. *Religious System of China*. 3:935–1056. Leiden, Netherlands: Brill, 1897.

Dehergne, Joseph. *Répertoire des Jésuites de Chine de 1552 à 1800*. Rome: Institutum Historicum Societatis Iesu, 1973.

Dudink, Adrian. "The Inventories of the Jesuit House at Nanking Made Up during the Persecution of 1616–1617 (Shen Que, *Nangong shudu*, 1620)." In *Western Humanistic Culture Presented to China by Jesuit Missionaries (Seventeenth and Eighteenth Centuries)*, edited by Federico Masini, 119–57. Rome: Institutum Historicum Societatis Iesu, 1996.

Eitel, Ernest J. *Feng-shui*. Singapore: Graham Brash, 1985. First published in the *Chinese Recorder and Missionary Journal*, March 1872.

Entenmann, Robert E. "Catholics and Society in Eighteenth-Century Sichuan." In *Christianity in China: From the Eighteenth Century to the Present*, edited by Daniel H. Bays, 8–23. Stanford, Calif.: Stanford University Press, 1966.

Fong, Wen. Review of James Cahill's *The Compelling Image*. *Art Bulletin* 68, no. 3 (September 1986): 504–8.

Foss, Theodore Nicholas. "The European Sojourn of Philippe Couplet and Michael Shen Fuzong, 1683–1692." In *Philippe Couplet, S.J. (1623–1693): The Man Who Brought China to Europe*, edited by Jerome Heyndrickx, 121–42. Nettetal, Germany: Steyler Verlag, 1990.

Fu, Lo-shu. *Documentary Chronicle of Sino-Western Relations (1644–1820)*. Tucson: University of Arizona Press, 1966.

Gernet, Jacques. *China and the Christian Impact: A Conflict of Cultures*. Translated by Janet Lloyd. Cambridge: Cambridge University Press, 1985.

Hsiang, Ta. "European Influences on Chinese Art in the Later Ming and Early Ch'ing Period." Translated by Wang Teh-chao. *Renditions* 6 (1976): 152–78.

Huang Yilong. *Liang tou xia: Ming mo Qing chu de diyi dai Tianzhujiao jiaotu* (Two-headed Snake: The First Christians of the Late Ming and Early Qing Dynasties). Xinzhu, Taiwan: National Tsing Hua University Press, 2005.

Hummel, Arthur, ed. *Eminent Chinese of the Ch'ing Period (1644–1912)*. Washington, D.C.: U.S. Government Printing Office, 1943.

Hwang, Jane. "The Early Jesuits' Printings in China in the Bavarian State Library and the University Library of Munich." In *Collected Essays of the International Symposium on Chinese-Western Cultural Interchange in Commemoration of the 400th Anniversary of the Arrival of Matteo Ricci, S.J., in China*, edited by Kuang Lo, 281–93. Taipei, Taiwan: Fu Jen, 1983.

Jennes, Jos. "L'art chrétien en Chine au début du dix-septième siècle (une gravure d'Antoine Wierx identifiée comme modèle d'une peinture de Tong K'i-tch'ang)." *T'oung Pao* 33 (1937): 129–33.

Kao, Mayching "European Influences in Chinese Art, Sixteenth to Eighteenth Centuries." In *China and Europe: Images and Influences in Sixteenth to Eighteenth Centuries*, edited by Thomas H. C. Lee, 251–81. Hong Kong: Chinese University Press, 1991.

King, Gail. "Couplet's Biography of Madame Candida Xu (1607–1680)." *Sino-Western Cultural Relations Journal* 18 (1996): 41–56.

———. "Note on a Late Ming Dynasty Chinese Description of 'Ricci's Church' in Beijing." *Sino-Western Cultural Relations Journal* 20 (1998): 49–51.

Kuhn, Philip A. *Soulstealers: The Chinese Sorcery Scare of 1768*. Cambridge, Mass.: Harvard University Press, 1990.

Laufer, Berthold. "Christian Art in China." *Mitteilungen des Seminars für Orientalische Sprachen* (1910): 100–118 plus plates.

Lindorff, Joyce A. "The Harpsichord and Clavichord in China during the Ming and Qing Dynasties." *Early Keyboard Studies Newsletter* 8, no. 4 (October 1994): 1–8.

Loehr, George. "Missionary-Artists at the Manchu Court." *Transactions of the Oriental Ceramic Society* (London) 34 (1962–1963): 51–67.

Marks, Robert B. *The Origins of the Modern World: A Global and Ecological Narrative from the Fifteenth to the Twenty-first Century*. 2nd ed. Lanham, Md.: Rowman & Littlefield, 2007.

McCall, John E. "Early Jesuit Art in the Far East. Part 4: In China and Macao before 1635." *Artibus Asiae* 11 (1949): 45–69.

Millward, James A. "A Uyghur Muslim in Qianlong's Court: The Meanings of the Fragrant Concubine." *Journal of Asian Studies* 53 (1994): 427–58.

Mungello, D. E. *Forgotten Christians of Hangzhou*. Honolulu: University of Hawaii Press, 1994.

———, ed. *The Rites Controversy: Its History and Meaning*. Nettetal, Germany: Steyler Verlag, 1994.

———. *The Spirit and the Flesh in Shandong, 1650–1785*. Lanham, Md.: Rowman & Littlefield, 2001.

Needham, Joseph. *Science and Civilisation in China*. 7 vols. in progress. Cambridge: Cambridge University Press, 1954– . See esp. vols. 2 and 3.

Pelliot, Paul. "Les 'Conquêtes de l'empereur de la Chine.'" *T'oung Pao* 20 (1921): 183–274.

———. "Les influences européennes sur l'art chinois au dix-septième et au dix-huitième siècle." Conférence faite au Musée Guimet le 20 février 1927. Paris: Imprimerie National, 1948.

———. "La peinture et la gravure européennes en Chine au temps de Mathieu Ricci." *T'oung Pao* 20 (1920–1921): 1–18.

Pfister, Louis. *Notices biographiques et bibliographiques sur les Jésuites de l'ancienne Mission de Chine, 1552–1773*. Shanghai: Mission Catholique, 1932–1934.

Rheinbay, Paul. "Nadal's Religious Iconography Reinterpreted by Aleni for China." In *Scholar from the West: Giulio Aleni S.J. (1582–1649) and the Dialogue between*

Christianity and China, edited by Tiziana Lippiello and Roman Malek, 323–34. Nettetal, Germany: Steyler Verlag, 1997.

Rosso, Antonio Sisto. *Apostolic Legations to China of the Eighteenth Century*. South Pasadena, Calif.: Perkins, 1948.

Spence, Jonathan S. *The Memory Palace of Matteo Ricci*. New York: Viking, 1984.

———. *The Question of Hu*. New York: Vintage, 1989.

Sullivan, Michael. "The Chinese Response to Western Art." *Art International* 24, nos. 3–4 (November–December 1980): 8–31.

———. *The Meeting of Eastern and Western Art from the Sixteenth Century to the Present Day*. New York: New York Graphic Society, 1973.

———. "Some Possible Sources of European Influence on Late Ming and Early Ch'ing Painting." In *Proceedings of the International Symposium on Chinese Painting*, 595–625 plus 9 plates. Taipei, Taiwan: Fu Jen, 1972.

Swiderski, Richard M. "The Dragon and the Straightedge: A Semiotics of the Chinese Response to European Pictorial Space." *Semiotica* 81, nos. 1–2 (1990): 1–41; 82, nos. 1–2 (1990): 43–136; and 82, nos. 3–4 (1990): 211–68.

Taixeira, Manuel. "The Church of St. Paul in Macau." *Studia* (Lisbon) 41–42 (1979): 51–111 plus 3 illustrations.

Vanderstappen, Harrie. "Chinese Art and the Jesuits in Peking." In *East Meets West: The Jesuits in China, 1582–1773*, edited by Charles E. Ronan and Bonnie B. C. Oh, 103–26. Chicago: Loyola University Press, 1988.

Verhaeren, H. *Catalogue de la bibliothèque du Pé-tang*. Beijing: Lazaristes, 1949.

———. "Ordonnances de la Sainte Eglise" (in French and Chinese). *Monumenta Serica* (Beijing) 4 (1939–1940): 451–77.

Voet, Leon. *The Golden Compasses: A History and Evaluation of the Printing and Publishing Activities of the Officina Plantiniana at Antwerp*. 2 vols. Amsterdam: Vangendt, 1972.

Waley, Arthur. "Ricci and Tung ch'i-ch'ang." *T'oung Pao* 2 (1922): 342–43.

Wu, Hung. "Emperor's Masquerade: 'Costume Portraits' of Yongzheng and Qianlong." *Orientations* (Hong Kong) 26 (1995): 25–41.

Young, John D. *Confucianism and Christianity: The First Encounter*. Hong Kong: University of Hong Kong Press, 1983.

Zürcher, E. *Bouddhisme: Christianisme et société chinoise*. Paris: Julliard, 1990.

———. "The First Anti-Christian Movement in China (Nanking, 1616–1621)." In *Acta Orientalia Neerlandica*, edited by P. W. Pestman, 188–95. Leiden, Netherlands: Brill, 1971.

———. "Giulio Aleni's Chinese Biography." In *Scholar from the West: Giulio Aleni S.J. (1582–1649) and the Dialogue between Christianity and China*, edited by Tiziana Lippiello and Roman Malek, 85–127. Nettetal, Germany: Steyler Verlag, 1997.

———. *Kuoduo richao, Li Jiubiao's Diary of Oral Admonitions: A Late Ming Christian Journal*. Translated, with introduction and notes, by Erik Zürcher. 2 vols. Nettetal, Germany: Steyler Verlag, 2007.

4

EUROPEAN ACCEPTANCE
OF CHINESE CULTURE
AND CONFUCIANISM

EARLY CHINESE VISITORS TO EUROPE

Why did Europeans admire Chinese culture, and why did they want to borrow the philosophy of Confucius? Europeans were influenced by China because they regarded Chinese culture as superior, and they were eager to borrow from China, at least until the end of the eighteenth century.

European admiration for Chinese culture was not based upon direct contact with Chinese. Most Europeans had never seen a Chinese person and knew only what they had heard or read about in the missionary-authored books on China, which were consumed in Europe with avid interest. Unlike in China where the number of European missionaries and traders during the period 1500–1800 amounted to several thousand, the number of Chinese (all males) who visited Europe probably amounted to no more than two or three hundred, and most of these went to Rome and Naples in church-related activities. Rare indeed was the appearance of a Chinese in northern Europe, even in major cities like London or Paris.

The first recorded instance of a Chinese in Europe dates from Portugal in 1540 or shortly thereafter. This Chinese had probably been taken prisoner and enslaved during one of the Portuguese raids of ports along the southeast coast of China in the first half of the sixteenth century. He was not a domestic servant but rather well educated and was bought in Portugal by the historian João de Barros to translate Chinese works into Portuguese since he was proficient in both languages. The next Chinese to visit Portugal came to Lisbon in 1755. He survived the great Lisbon earthquake and went to England in 1756. An engraving of this Loum Riqua by Dominique Serres was published in London in 1787.

One of the earliest well-documented voyages of a Chinese to Europe was that of Shen Fuzong (b. 1658), baptized Michael Alphonse. The Jesuit Father Philippe Couplet (1623–1693) met Shen's father, a prominent Chinese Christian physician, while working in Jiangsu province in the lower Yangzi River region. Couplet was preparing to return to Europe to drum up support for the China Mission, and his superiors decided that the effort would be aided by taking several Chinese candidates for the priesthood. Of the five candidates that they originally intended to send, Shen was the only one who reached Europe.

Unlike a handful of the visits of earlier Chinese brought to Europe by missionaries, Shen's visit received a great deal of attention. After a long, two-year journey, Couplet and Shen arrived in Holland in October of 1683. Couplet consciously made use of Shen's exotic qualities, including his Chinese clothing, in an effort to attract support for the mission. Shen was taught enough Latin to communicate. In Paris they attracted a crowd when they said mass at Montmartre. At Versailles, Louis XIV was fascinated by Shen eating with little ivory chopsticks and, in an unusual display of favor, had all the fountains turned on. In Rome in 1685, Couplet and Shen met with Pope Innocent XI. In London in 1687 they were given a royal reception by King James II, who was so intrigued by Shen that he ordered Sir Godfrey Kneller to paint a portrait of him in Chinese dress (see figure 4.1). Shen entered the novitiate in Lisbon and took his first vows in 1690. However, he never saw his homeland again; en route back to China in 1691, he died from an epidemic.

Shen's voyage to Europe was very successful in promoting European interest and support of the Jesuit mission in China. However, sometimes, visits of Chinese to Europe turned out disastrously. Much depended on the motivation of the Chinese and his relationship to the priest he accompanied. If the Chinese was very dedicated to becoming a priest and had a strong bond to the priest who brought him, the journey tended to be successful. But if the spiritual calling (vocation) of the Chinese was less strong and the commitment of the priest who accompanied him tepid, disaster could result.

Fan Shouyi (1682–1753) was exemplary in his devotion to the priest who brought him to Europe. In 1709 Fan left his remote home in Jiangzhou, in Shanxi province, to follow his spiritual mentor, the Jesuit Father Francesco Giuseppe Provana, to Rome. Later he followed Provana to his home in Turin and nursed him back to health. Provana had been sent by the Kangxi Emperor to Rome on a mission, and the pope now sent him back on a mission to China. When Provana died in 1720 while at sea near the Cape of Good

Figure 4.1. "The Chinese Convert" (Michael Shen Fuzong), oil on canvas, dated 1687, by Sir Godfrey Kneller. Kensington Palace, London. Permission of the Royal Collection © 2004, Her Majesty Queen Elizabeth II. Shen, a Chinese candidate for the priesthood, was brought to Europe by the Jesuit Father Philippe Couplet. While they were visiting London in 1687, King James II was so intrigued by Shen that he ordered this portrait to be painted and to be hung near his bedchamber.

Hope, Fan refused to abandon his master to burial at sea but with great devotion saw that the body was taken back to China to be buried in consecrated ground. Fan was greeted at his arrival in Macau by imperial troops and summoned to Beijing for an imperial audience. He was later ordained as a Jesuit. Fan Shouyi, along with the painter-poet Wu Li, were among the relatively few Chinese of that time to attain the priesthood. The small number of ordinations was due, in part, to the tremendous obstacles to learning the ritualized Latin of the church and, in part, to the reluctance of European religious authorities to entrust the church to native clergy.

The journey of John Hu (ca. 1681–after 1726) of Canton to Europe was as disastrous as Fan's journey was glorious. Hu had been baptized at the age of nineteen with the name of John (Ruowang). He was already forty years old (whereas Fan had been twenty-seven) when he departed for Europe. In Canton, he served as keeper of the gate, a kind of majordomo, of the Propaganda residence. Although it was a position of responsibility, it probably was a terminal appointment because there were no plans for Hu to become a priest. He was literate in Chinese (keeping a written record of visitors to the Propaganda residence was one of his tasks), though not learned enough to be admitted to the ranks of the literati. He was a widower with one grown son. He also served as a catechist in the Propaganda church in Canton.

In 1720 the Jesuit Father Jean-François Foucquet of Beijing finally received, after many petitions, permission to return to Europe, but he had to depart in eight days. Foucquet had amassed a large library of Chinese books, hoping to prove that the most ancient Chinese texts, particularly the *Book of Changes*, had anticipated the revelation of Jesus Christ. This theory, called Figurism because it made a figurative rather than a literal interpretation of the Chinese classics, was controversial and shared by only a few Jesuits. Foucquet quickly packed several thousand of his volumes (many volumes had to be left behind) on sixteen mules and traveled south to Canton.

While awaiting a ship in Canton, Foucquet tried to find a scribe who could accompany him to Europe to copy Chinese texts. John Hu was presented to him, but Foucquet was not entirely satisfied with him. Nevertheless, given the urgency of his departure and the lack of other candidates, Foucquet and Hu signed a five-year contract under which Hu was to copy Chinese texts from Foucquet's collection in return for twenty taels of silver each year, plus the cost of his food and passage. Soon after departure, Hu began to manifest some of the irrational behavior that would become so pronounced after his arrival in Europe. He had visions and began to rebel against Foucquet's authority.

Whereas Couplet and Provana had selected their Chinese companions in a teacher-student relationship where the student would one day succeed the teacher, Foucquet saw Hu merely as an employee. A contract would have been completely inappropriate for Shen Fuzong and Fan Shouyi, but the money was important for Hu, whose life was driven by more mundane concerns. Because Foucquet viewed Hu as only a scribe, he did not teach Hu any European language. This had the unfortunate and disastrous result of making Hu totally dependent on Foucquet for communication in Europe.

The lack of communication with people in his new world appears to have exacerbated Hu's erratic behavior. He jumped from a moving carriage to pick wild berries, and he gave away his expensive new clothes to a beggar. He became sullen and began to refuse to assist Foucquet in serving mass. He was offended by the presence of women in the European churches. He refused to copy any texts for Foucquet. He took food at will and disappeared for a week. As his behavior became more erratic and uncontrollable, Foucquet sought to detach himself from Hu. Eventually, Hu was sent to an insane asylum in the hospital of Charenton, where, because the fees for his stay were never paid, he became a charity case. The clothes he wore disintegrated and were not replaced. Finally, in 1725, after Hu had spent almost two years of incarceration at Charenton, another Jesuit who had known him in Canton and who disliked Foucquet appeared and secured his passage home to Canton, where he arrived in November of 1726. Although he had not done the work of scribe stipulated in his contract, he complained loudly to the head of the Propaganda house in Canton until he was paid.

CHINESE RITES CONTROVERSY FROM THE EUROPEAN PERSPECTIVE

The positive reaction of Europeans to Chinese culture and philosophy was the result, first of all, of the religious impulse exemplified by the Catholic missionaries in China, who provided the first substantive information about Chinese culture to Europe. This information was shaped by the Jesuits' realistic assessment that China was in many ways, apart from its lack of Christianity, the equal or superior of Europe. The Jesuits recognized that the Chinese, unlike those in other less technologically or materially advanced parts of the world, could not be converted by overawing them by European might. Rather, the Chinese needed to be approached as intellectual equals and shown through sophisticated argument that Christianity was in harmony with some of their most fundamental beliefs.

The Jesuits were not alone among Christian missionaries in admiring China. One of the leading critics of the Jesuits, the Spanish Dominican Domingo Navarrete (1618–1686), repeatedly said that the Chinese surpassed all other nations in the world. Nevertheless, the Jesuits were more accommodating than other missionaries in attempting to reconcile Christianity with Chinese culture. Because the Jesuits' closest Chinese counterparts in terms of education, social standing, and moral cultivation were the Confucian literati, the Jesuits cultivated the literati and presented them in a highly favorable light to Europeans. Conversely, Buddhism and Daoism were slighted. Realizing that these teachings were less compatible with Christianity, the Jesuits presented Buddhism and Daoism in a highly disparaging way and emphasized their superstitious qualities. Not until the nineteenth century would Buddhism receive more objective treatment from scholars in the West.

Since it was necessary to justify their accommodationist plan in Europe, the Jesuits worked to develop the idea that a form of natural religion existed in China. They claimed that Confucianism contained truths derived from the natural world and human reason and lacked only the truths of revelation. The dominant Jesuit view argued that most moral and social truths of Confucianism, such as honoring one's parents and treating others as we ourselves would wish to be treated, were similar to Christianity. Elements of Confucianism that conflicted with Christianity, including certain superstitious rites to deceased ancestors and the practice of polygamy, would have to be abandoned prior to baptism. Confucius was presented as a teacher and scholar rather than a religious leader. This view led the Jesuits to undertake a Latin translation of the Confucian Four Books (*The Great Learning, Doctrine of the Mean, Analects of Confucius*, and *Mencius*). These four works were the primary texts of the Chinese educational curriculum. The translation project was initiated in China in the 1580s when Jesuits began using their tentative translations of these important texts as Chinese-language primers for teaching newly arrived Jesuits. These translations were handed down and improved over the years until finally they were carried back to Europe and published in a series of works that culminated in 1711. The most influential of these Jesuit translations was *Confucius, Philosopher of the Chinese* (*Confucius Sinarum Philosophus*; Paris, 1687; see figure 1.1). These translations were widely read in Europe, and their sympathetic portrayal of Confucius was very influential.

The Jesuits succeeded in presenting Confucianism as a philosophy that was very appealing to the cultural needs of Europe in the seventeenth and eighteenth centuries. Although Confucianism lacked the divine revelation of

Christianity, it was otherwise complementary to Christianity and could be used to elaborate and enrich the teachings of Christianity in the way that Greek philosophy had been used by the early church. The charity of the Chinese was compared to the charity of Christians. In fact, the reconciliation of pagan Greek and Roman authors with Christianity by Renaissance humanists provided a precedent for the reconciliation of Chinese philosophy by Christians of the seventeenth century. The Jesuits' argument was persuasive in a way that boomeranged on them. Later, in eighteenth-century France, the teachings of Confucius were taken up by anti-Christian thinkers of the Enlightenment and presented as an admirable philosophy precisely because it *lacked* divine revelation. The deism and benevolent despotism of Chinese monarchs seemed admirable models of what Enlightenment thinkers were promoting in Europe. Other leading European intellects of the time, such as the German Gottfried Wilhelm Leibniz (1646–1716), found in Confucian philosophy confirmation of universal truths that they had discovered in their own research.

The presentation of this accommodating interpretation of Confucianism became entangled with the previously discussed struggle among European Christians called the Chinese Rites Controversy. The most important rites involved were rituals performed in honor of ancestors and Confucius. Some missionaries claimed that these rites involved worship of Confucius and ancestral spirits as idols. While conceding that certain rites to ancestors were superstitions, the Jesuits argued—with the assistance of literati converts—that the rites to ancestors had an essentially social and moral significance. They did not violate the monotheistic nature of the Christian God because, the Jesuits said—though other Christians disagreed—the Chinese were not praying to their ancestors for benefits from beyond the grave. The Jesuits prohibited their converts from practicing certain rites to Confucius but allowed others on the grounds that these rites were more civil than religious in nature. A related debate raged over the Chinese terms for God. Whereas many missionaries felt traditional Chinese terms for God, such as *Shangdi* (Lord-on-High) and *Tian* (Heaven), were tainted because they had been used in ancient, pre-Christian texts, the Jesuits used these traditional terms in an attempt to accommodate Christianity with Chinese culture. The use of the terms showed that Christianity was not alien to Chinese culture even though the meaning of the terms needed to be fine-tuned to fit the exact meaning of Christianity. As an acceptable, untainted alternative, the Jesuits proposed that a new term, *Tianzhu* (Lord of Heaven), be used.

The Chinese Rites Controversy involved many people and much bitterness. The Jesuits, who were the leading proponents of accommodation, lost this battle temporarily. As a result, the Jesuit interpretation of Confucianism was discredited, and accommodation was rejected by Catholic authorities in Rome in 1704, a rejection that was later confirmed by papal decrees of 1715 and 1742. (Much later, in 1939, this rejection was reversed by Rome on the grounds that similar Japanese Shinto rites were more civil and social than religious in nature.) Those sympathetic to Jesuit accommodation viewed the eighteenth-century rejection of accommodation as an important turning point in the history of Christianity of China. But this interpretation betrays a kind of chauvinism in that it portrays Europeans as the primary actors in this struggle and the Chinese as passive responders. The initial growth of Christianity in China in the early seventeenth century stagnated only in part because European Christians became less accommodating. The stagnation was also due to an active rejection of Christianity by Chinese on grounds that were independent of what the Europeans did. Clearly, however, Rome's prohibition of further debate of Rites Controversy issues had a chilling effect on Confucian-Christian dialogue, and to that extent it damaged the effort to inculturate Christianity in China.

THE PROTO-SINOLOGISTS

Missions to China were expensive and funding was always a problem. The Jesuits attempted to shape European public opinion in a way favorable to their missionary approach in China and tried to gain the support of royal or commercial patrons who would support their missions. The relative poverty of early modern Europe in comparison with China is shown in this preoccupation with funding. Early in the Ming dynasty, the Yongle Emperor underwrote the costs of a series of seven enormous expeditions led by the eunuch Zheng He. Some of these consisted of over three hundred ships and twenty-eight thousand men and ventured into the Indian Ocean and as far as east Africa in the years 1404–1433 (see map 1). Such grand voyages would have been impossibly beyond the means of any European monarch of that time. One of the more elaborate European missions of the seventeenth century was the group of six Jesuits organized in 1685 in part by the French Academy of Sciences and subsidized by Louis XIV (r. 1643–1715).

Through Europe's enthusiastic response to the Jesuits' presentations, China entered the realm of popular European culture in the early seventeenth century. Popular culture is often grounded in less substantive concerns and so is more subject to the shifting tides of fashion, whether fashionable ideas or fashionable artistic tastes. Unlike the more serious study of

China by scholars of that time, the popular interest in China in the seventeenth and eighteenth centuries took the form of enthusiasms that were subject to wide and sudden swings of support.

The scholarly study of China was made by a relatively small group of intellectuals. Given the commitment needed to study the Chinese language and culture, such scholars took a serious approach to China. The seventeenth- and eighteenth-century model in scholarship was that of a polyhistor (or polymath) rather than a specialist. Polyhistors tried to acquire knowledge in as many fields as possible rather than expertise in only one field. They were less specialized than today's experts but were far from being mere amateurs.

The polyhistor style of scholarship culminated in Leibniz. Contemporary scholarship, which prizes expertise in a particular area of knowledge, has difficulty dealing with a polyhistor like Leibniz. The tendency is to view him as having expertise in several areas, preeminently philosophy and mathematics, but such a classification misses the point. Leibniz would have regarded such classification of his work as demeaning, because his age prized the ability to move with learned ease through as many fields as possible. Leibniz's polyhistor style of scholarship is not something easily detached from his achievements in philosophy because it could be argued (and probably would have been argued by seventeenth-century savants) that his philosophic insights were the result of the breadth of his knowledge. This breadth enabled him to see connections or overarching patterns linking these different areas. He worked in diverse fields, writing a history of the house of Braunschweig, directing the Herzog August Library in Wolfenbüttel, managing a Harz Mountain mine, conducting negotiations of reconciliation between Catholics and Protestants, producing a mechanical calculator, and inventing the calculus.

We use the term "proto-Sinologists" to distinguish early students of China from later China scholars. Some of their ideas about Chinese language and culture may have been false, and even ridiculous, but their interest in China was less vulnerable to the tides of intellectual fashion than that of the popularizers of their time. One such proto-Sinological idea was the belief in a *Clavis Sinica*, or "key" to Chinese, that would enable one to radically simplify and reduce the amount of study needed to master the Chinese language. The notion of developing such a key was based upon the belief that it was possible to have a single universal language. The European discovery of many unknown languages in Asia had revived the idea of the biblical proliferation of tongues at Babel (Genesis 11:1–9), which was believed to have ended the universality of the Primitive Language given by

God to Adam (Genesis 2:19–20). One school of thought believed that once this common structure was rediscovered, the results could be applied to understanding other languages, such as Chinese. Some believed that Chinese *was* the Primitive Language that had existed prior to the confusion of tongues.

Another school of thought held that, while it would be impossible to recover the Primitive Language, it would be possible to create a new universal language, using principles such as Real Characters. Real Characters involved writing that represents not merely letters or words but also things and ideas. Since Real Characters are not arbitrary signs, they need not be learned but rather convey their meaning in a manner that is universally understood. Leibniz believed that the Chinese language contained Real Characters. All this was part of the seventeenth-century search for a universal language. Clearly there is a universalism operative here that may in some ways be naive but that in other ways reveals an egalitarianism (but not relativism) among cultures that predates the development of ideas about European cultural superiority.

While the notion of such a key to Chinese may strike us today as preposterous, it was taken seriously by many intellectuals of that time because it was reinforced by certain widely held ideas about the development of languages. Frederick William, the Great Elector of Prussia (r. 1640–1688), like many minor princes, dreamt of the wealth to be obtained through the founding of an East India trading company, and to this end he supported proto-Sinological research. In 1674, a member of his Berlin court, the Lutheran pastor Andreas Müller (1630–1694), announced his discovery of such a key in a four-page pamphlet entitled "Proposal on a Key Suitable for Chinese" (*Propositio super clave sua Sinica*). Müller promised to release this key upon the payment of a fee—half in advance paid into an escrow account and the remaining half upon delivery. Unfortunately, Müller's key was never revealed.

It appears that Müller's announcement of a Clavis Sinica represented a research proposal in search of funding rather than a finalized technique available for purchase. Müller's precarious position (because of theological tensions between Lutherans and Calvinists) at the Brandenburg-Berlin court, combined with the needs of supporting a large family and the frequent delay in the payment of salaries at the financially strapped court, made his demand for an advance payment less cynical than it might appear today. In addition, Müller had incurred debts through the expense of producing a wooden typeset of Chinese characters. This typographia consisted of small wooden blocks upon each of which one character was engraved. These

3,284 blocks have survived and may be found in the Berlin Staatsbibliothek today. It seems that Müller had an idea for developing such a key based upon applying musical notation to reproduce the tones of the Chinese language, but his key was not yet fully developed because he needed financial support to complete it. In the face of understandable requests from scholars for information on his key, Müller steadfastly refused to divulge any information until the fee was paid. Just before his death, after having been discharged from his position at the Berlin court, a discouraged and embittered Müller burned his manuscripts. Yet the idea of a Clavis Sinica lived on.

The responses among European intellectuals to such a key were mixed. One of the scholarly stars of that age, the prolific German-born Jesuit Athanasius Kircher (1602–1680), was doubtful about the possibility of constructing such a key. However, one of the most brilliant men of his time, Leibniz, was interested and addressed a number of questions to Müller that were never answered (and could not have been answered given the incomplete state of Müller's research). However, in 1697, when Müller's proto-Sinological successor at Berlin, the physician Christian Mentzel (1622–1701), also claimed to have developed a Clavis Sinica, Leibniz was enthusiastic. Although Mentzel's key was never presented in its entirety, several pages of it were published. They show that it was based on the lexical work *Zihui* (1615) of a Chinese scholar Mei Yingzuo (1570–1615) and on a dictionary that was organized on Mei's principles. Mei had classified the Chinese characters according to 214 radicals, or classifiers (see figure 4.2). Since Chinese lacks an alphabet and cannot be arranged in alphabetical order, these 214 radicals proved crucial in organizing and classifying the characters. However, Mentzel saw the 214-radical system as more than an artificial lexical arrangement and in fact believed that these categories revealed the underlying structure of the Chinese written language. Gradually over the seventeenth and eighteenth centuries, the meaning of a Clavis Sinica evolved from being a shortcut to learning Chinese (Müller) to a translation aid (Mentzel) and finally to a Chinese grammar.

The story of the Clavis Sinica shows how far China penetrated into European culture. In the late seventeenth century, Brandenburg-Berlin was a political and intellectual backwater. Scholars like Müller and Mentzel were overshadowed by eminent savants like Kircher and Leibniz. Unlike Rome or Paris, Brandenburg-Berlin rarely saw a missionary from China. And yet the Great Elector Frederick William had great hopes for his kingdom, and China was viewed as having a part in that greatness. Consequently, the Great Elector encouraged the work of proto-Sinologists like Müller and Mentzel to gather information on China's language, geography, botany, medicines,

辭源修訂本部首目錄

子集		女	728	方	1379	生	2095	色	2610	韋	3372
一畫		寅集		无	1396	用	2100	申集		韭	3377
一	1	子	773	辰集		田	2101	艸艹同	2613	音	3377
丨	83	宀	799	日	1396	疋疋同	2128	虍	2746	頁	3381
丶	93	寸	867	曰	1455	疒	2132	虫	2756	風	3404
丿	97	小	882	月	1472	癶	2149	血	2797	飛	3415
乙	101	尢兀同	898	木	1493	白	2155	行	2799	食	3420
亅	120	尸	900	欠	1651	皮	2182	衣礻同	2811	首	3437
二畫		屮	917	止	1661	皿	2184	襾	2840	香	3439
二	122	山	918	歹	1680	目罒同	2197	酉集		亥集	
亠	148	巛	949	殳	1687	矛	2225	七畫		十畫	
人	158	工	952	毋	1692	矢	2227	見	2852	馬	3443
儿	268	己	963	比	1694	石	2232	角	2862	骨	3471
入	284	巾	966	毛	1697	示礻	2262	言	2872	高	3477
八	296	干	988	氏	1702	内	2290	谷	2928	髟	3485
冂	320	幺	999	气	1704	禾	2292	豆	2929	鬥	3490
冖	322	广	1003	巳集		穴	2321	豕	2934	鬯	3492
冫	325	廴	1028	水氵冰同	1707	立	2335	豸	2941	鬲	3494
几	332	廾	1034	火灬同	1908	冰同水		貝	2946	鬼	3495
凵	333	弋	1036	爪爫同	1965	疋同疋		赤	2976	十一畫	
刀	337	弓	1037	父	1968	罒同目		走	2982	魚	3502
力	371	彐	1059	爻	1969	礻同衣		足	2991	鳥	3520
勹	385	彡	1060	爿	1971	未集		身	3011	鹵	3551
匕	388	彳	1067	片	1972	六畫		車	3013	鹿	3554
匚	393	兀同尢		牙	1975	竹	2344	辛	3037	麥	3561
匸	395	彑同彐		牛牜同	1978	米	2382	辰	3043	麻	3564
十	397	ヨ同彐		犬同犭	1992	糸	2394	辵辶同	3045	十二畫	
卜	430	忄同心				缶	2478	邑右阝同	3096	黃	3566
卩	432	扌同手				网罒冖同	2480	酉	3127	黍	3576
厂	439	氵同水				羊	2490	釆	3143	黑	3577
厶	443	犭同犬				羽	2502	里	3146	黹	3586
又	447	阝在右同邑				老	2515	戌集		十三畫	
亻同人	158	阝在左同阜				而	2522	八畫		黽	3587
刂同刀	337	辶同辵				耒	2523	金	3155	鼎	3589
㔾同卩	432	卯集				耳	2526	長	3223	鼓	3591
丑集		四畫				聿	2539	門	3231	鼠	3593
三畫		心	1093			肉月同	2541	阜左阝同	3257	十四畫	
口	455	戈	1182	午集		臣	2577	隶	3300	鼻	3595
囗	559	户	1197	五畫		自	2582	隹	3301	齊	3597
土	582	手	1203	玄	2018	至	2587	雨	3324	十五畫	
士	639	支	1331	玉王同	2027	臼	2590	青	3349	齒	3601
夂	645	攴	1333	瓜	2081	舌	2597	非	3359	十六畫	
夊	645	文	1356	瓦	2084	舛	2600	九畫		龍	3605
夕	649	斗	1367	甘	2091	舟	2602	面	3362	龜	3617
大	660	斤	1371			艮	2607	革	3364	十七畫	
										龠	3620

Figure 4.2. The 214 radicals (classifiers) of the Chinese written language, first formulated by Mei Yingzuo (1570–1615). Reproduced from the dictionary *Ziyuan* (Shanghai, 1915; revised Beijing, 1983). The Chinese written language is not based upon an alphabet, and these radicals have been the primary basis for organizing characters in Chinese dictionaries for the past four hundred years.

history, and literature. As a result, an impressive early collection of Chinese books was amassed in Berlin along with Müller's typographia of wooden blocks of Chinese characters. The story of the Clavis Sinica also teaches us that the intellectual world of that time in Europe was far more cosmopolitan in outlook than we sometimes think.

Additional evidence for the lack of European cultural superiority in the seventeenth century is shown by the intellectual challenge that China's history posed to European identity. Whereas theology was known as the queen of the sciences in Europe, in China this role was occupied by history. China's experience as the longest continuous civilization in the world has fostered a historical scholarship unparalleled in any other culture. Seventeenth-century Europe had a passion for precise chronologies, and that passion was inevitably tied to the Bible. In 1650–1654 in London, the Anglican archbishop James Ussher published a chronology in Latin entitled *Annals of the Old and New Testaments* in which he dated the creation of Adam to 4004 BC and the Noachian flood to 2349 BC. Ussher's dates became so widely accepted that they were inserted into the margins of reference editions of the King James version of the Bible.

Less than ten years after the publication of Ussher's book, the Jesuit missionary Martino Martini returned from China and published the first edition in Latin of his work on Chinese history, *The First Ten Divisions of Chinese History (Sinicae historiae decas prima res;* Munich, 1658). This was the first genuine history of China to appear in a European language (though it concluded at 1 BC). Drawing from Chinese historical records, Martini dated the beginning of Chinese history from Fu Xi in 2952 BC. He also followed Chinese scholars in eliminating numerous legendary events, including several creation myths, and beginning the historical record with Fu Xi. Anti-Jesuit feeling in Europe was so strong that some Europeans dismissed China's historical longevity as a myth created by the Jesuits for their own ends; however, many others accepted the claim of China's high antiquity.

The challenge to Ussher's chronology that Martini's book raised was immediately apparent. In the seventeenth-century biblical view of human history, Noah was the father of all mankind because everyone, apart from Noah and his descendants, was thought to have been killed at the time of the Flood. However, if the Chinese could trace their history from a point in time before the Flood, then the claim of Noah's universal patriarchy was destroyed because there would have been another line of human descent. If the Flood did not occur until 2349 BC and if the Chinese could date their history from 2952 BC, then either Noah was not the father of mankind or one of the chronologies was wrong.

Martini and others immediately saw the solution, but it required a change in the biblical dating. Ussher's dates were supported by the fourth-century Vulgate version of the Bible, which was a Latin translation by Saint Jerome (ca. 347–420?) based on now lost Hebrew texts. However, there was an older translation of the Old Testament, the Septuagint, a Greek translation allegedly made by seventy-two scholars at Alexandria under the reign of Ptolemy Philadelphus (285–246 BC). One biblical chronology suggested by the Septuagint placed the Creation at 5200 BC and the Flood at 2957 BC, or five years prior to the beginning of Chinese history at 2952 BC. Adopting this would preserve Noah's universal patrimony. Although controversy would continue over the dating of biblical events, the debate shows how European culture was intellectually challenged by China. In the process, Chinese history was integrated into European "universal history" based on Old Testament–derived chronologies.

The way in which Jesuit publications on China, such as Martini's history, influenced European popular culture is shown in the case of John Webb (1611–1672) of England. Webb was an architect and antiquarian who published a book entitled *An Historical Essay Endeavoring a Probability That the Language of the Empire of China Is the Primitive Language* (London, 1669). Although he did not seriously study the Chinese language, Webb did read widely in the books on China, mainly by Jesuits, published in Europe, and he attempted to reconcile biblical and Chinese history. Webb claimed that the descendants of Noah (specifically the descendants of Shem, one of Noah's three sons) had migrated to China and thereby had preserved the Primitive Language. On the basis of the parallels Martini had drawn between the biblical Flood and the flood said to have occurred in China during the time of King Yao, Webb hypothesized that Noah and Yao were identical and that the Flood was worldwide.

CHINA POPULARIZERS IN EUROPE

To appreciate the different depths to which China penetrated the cultural interests of Europe in the seventeenth and eighteenth centuries, it is important to distinguish three levels of Europeans who studied and published books on China. The first level consisted of missionaries, mainly Jesuits, who had years of firsthand experience in China studying the difficult Chinese language and making contact with the Chinese.

The second level consisted of proto-Sinologists, who had a serious but less focused interest in China than the missionaries. Many of the proto-Sinologists believed in some common, universal basis of languages. This led, in the seventeenth century, to the belief that Chinese was perhaps the Biblical Primitive Language that existed prior to the multiplication of tongues at Babel and to Leibniz's view that Chinese contained Real Characters that could communicate on a universal scale. Other proto-Sinologists postulated some remarkable similarities between Chinese and several eastern Mediterranean languages and cultures. However, they had a Middle Eastern bias that led them to see knowledge spreading from the Middle East to China rather than the reverse. Athanasius Kircher, writing from Rome, believed that Egyptian culture had been disseminated to China by way of Noah's son Ham (rather than Shem or Japheth; Genesis 10). On this basis, Kircher claimed the Egyptian hieroglyphs were more ancient, purer, and deeper in hidden meaning than the Chinese characters. Kircher and other so-called disseminationists were too rooted in Middle Eastern studies to conclude that the flow of influence might have moved from China to the West.

The third level of Europeans with an interest in China consisted of those who were essentially popularizers, and they came to dominate the eighteenth-century view of China. They were interested neither in a cultural accommodation between Chinese and European cultures as part of a missionary strategy, as were the Jesuits, nor in a serious, intellectual approach that would yield advances in knowledge, whether it be the Clavis Sinica of Müller and Mentzel or the creation of universal forms of knowledge pursued by Leibniz. Rather, Europeans on this third level were interested in finding in China support for European political and intellectual movements, particularly the Enlightenment. This was the most superficial of the three levels of interest in China, and it produced the greatest distortions of Chinese culture. In short, European knowledge of China over the years 1500–1800 did not continue to evolve but rather after 1700 degenerated into the superficialities of exploitation by a European cultural movement (the Enlightenment) followed by a negative reaction against this superficial image of China.

Travel literature was in great vogue during the seventeenth and eighteenth centuries. Part of the interest was based on curiosity about unusual and remarkable lands and people, much like the interest in science fiction in our own age. But there was also a practical side to this interest because the information gained from travel literature was also useful to commerce. The new societies of learning in Europe, such as the Royal Society of London, combined intellectual and commercial interests. And yet European knowledge of China was so limited that it was possible for an imposter like George Psalmanazar (1679–1763) to succeed in meeting with the Royal Society in 1703 and (for a time) to be accepted as a native of Taiwan (Formosa). His book, *An Historical and Geographical Description of Formosa*, appeared in London bookshops in 1704 and immediately became a best seller in England, France, Germany, and Holland, although it was a complete fabrication written by someone who had never been to East Asia.

Psalmanazar's book was written in a style favored by that time for travel literature, namely, a colorful first-person account with many illustrations. It combined a description of an exotic land and people with a polemical attack on the Jesuits, which, in the overheated atmosphere of the Rites Controversy, played well with the many enemies of the Jesuits. The illustrations included a map of Formosa that bears only the most general likeness to reality. Psalmanazar described in detail an invented language that he called Formosan and presented illustrations of Formosans who looked remarkably European. He included drawings that supposedly depicted a Formosan funeral and emphasized the idolatry and human sacrifices of the Formosan religion, whose god (embodied in the form of an ox or elephant) demanded the hearts of eighteen thousand young boys every year. Fittingly, it was the Jesuits who eventually unmasked Psalmanazar as an imposter.

Louis Cousin (1627–1707) of France had been destined for service in the church, but after studying theology and law he secured a sinecure as the presiding officer at the Court of the Mint in 1659. This position gave him a secure income in return for few duties and enabled him to concentrate on his intellectual interests. In 1687 he became editor of one of the earliest periodicals, the *Journal des Savants*, to which he contributed until 1701. Academic honors came in 1697 with his election to the French Academy. As editor of the *Journal des Savants*, Cousin handled many reports and book reviews dealing with China. When *Confucius Sinarum Philosophus* was published in 1687, Cousin appears to have seen a potential for a broader readership by translating the work from scholarly Latin into more readable French and condensing it to more popular dimensions. (One must emphasize that he is only the apparent author because this condensed work was, like many works of that time in Europe, published anonymously, and Cousin's authorship is probable rather than definite.)

The resulting work, *The Morality of Confucius* (*La morale de Confucius*), was published in Amsterdam in 1688, only one year after the appearance of *Confucius Sinarum Philosophus*. The fact that the Jesuits had labored on their translation for a century reflects some of the differences between how these two levels of Europeans with an interest in China (the missionaries and the popularizers) approached their field. Although Cousin distorted the historical Confucius by exaggerating his rational qualities, he was merely reproducing the overly rationalized image of Confucianism presented in *Confucius Sinarum Philosophus*.

The same could not be said of another popularized work about Confucius. The Frenchman Nicolas-Gabriel Clerc (1726–1798) continued a family tradition in medicine by becoming a physician to eminent noblemen and their military units. In 1778 he was called to Versailles to become national inspector general of hospitals. Whereas Cousin occupied a largely literary world, Clerc moved in the highest political and social circles of the ancien régime in France and Russia. When the French Revolution began, Clerc turned to literary studies and especially to writing a six-volume history of Russia. His concern with moral nurturing on the very highest political and social level was reflected in his sole publication on China in 1769. *Yu the Great and Confucius: A Chinese history* (*Yu le Grand et Confucius, histoire chinoise*) was dedicated to the Grand Duke of Russia (later Czar Paul I, who was assassinated in 1801). Given the dedication, it is perhaps not surprising that in the very year of the book's publication Clerc received a dual appointment in Russia as physician to the Grand Duke Paul and director of the corps of cadets. In his dedication to *Yu the Great and Confucius*, Clerc exhorted the fifteen-year-old czarevitch to emulate the model of the ancient Chinese figure Yu the Great as the "prototype of morals of his nation." Clerc presented Yu as the father of his subjects who through his own behavior made the Chinese virtuous. Clerc reinforced his royal exhortation by noting that both Russia and China ruled vast territories.

What is striking about this book is the frank manner in which Clerc admits to fictionalizing Chinese history. Yao, Shun, and Yu were a famous trio of rulers in Chinese antiquity who were said to have established the principle of selecting rulers on the basis of morality and ability rather than birth. Clerc was aware that Yao, Shun, and Yu were three separate kings, yet he attributed actions of all three to Yu. (Most scholars today believe that these three kings were legendary rather than historical, but they were presented by most European sources of Clerc's time as historical.) Next, by treating Yu and Confucius as contemporaries, Clerc created an anachronism. He knew that approximately seventeen hundred years separated the lives of Yu the Great (r. 2205–2198 BC) and Confucius (551–479 BC), although he believed that the reader would excuse his fiction because of its necessity to the plan of his work. Another way in which Clerc fictionalized history was by choosing a legendary figure like Yu the Great, about whom very little was known, and then fabricating details about his life. The fact that much more was known about Confucius was not significant to Clerc, who was less interested in presenting the historical details of these two figures than in using them as models for the didactic instruction of the young Russian prince.

His delineation of Yu the Great and Confucius as models ("the best prince and the greatest philosopher of the Empire of China") reveals how much Clerc shared the values of the Enlightenment. Clerc presented them as models who exemplified one of the central tenets of that movement: to improve men, it is necessary only to enlighten them. Implicit in this statement is the assumption that knowledge by itself would lead to moral improvement. However, this is not exactly what Confucius taught. Clerc presented Confucius as a teacher of virtue, but he misinterpreted Confucian love as being egalitarian and universal in the Christian manner when in fact it is carefully defined by gradations of age and familial relationship. Clerc described the process by which Yu came to the throne as something very much like the philosophes' enlightened monarch consulting with an intellectual. Specifically, the legendary emperor Shun was said to have invited Confucius to share his crown. Confucius modestly declined that honor and recommended to Shun the name of Yu, whom Confucius regarded as the most worthy man in Shun's realm. When Yu attempted to decline on grounds of inability, Shun granted him a four-year grace period so he could be instructed by Confucius. This, of course, happened only in Clerc's fictionalized account.

LEIBNIZ, BOUVET, AND FIGURISM

Leibniz stands out as a monumental European figure whose understanding of Chinese culture was remarkably sophisticated for his age. He not only avidly read the books on China published in Europe but also initiated direct contact, mainly through correspondence, with Jesuits in China. In his famous introduction to *The Latest News of China* (*Novissima Sinica*; 1697), Leibniz wrote that Europeans surpassed the Chinese in the contemplative sciences and were the equals of the Chinese in technology. However, he said that Europeans were, in turn, surpassed by the Chinese in practical philosophy, by which he meant the adaptation of ethics and politics to contemporary life. Leibniz feared that Europe would be at a disadvantage to China if the exchange of missionaries between the two countries were not reciprocal. He advocated that Christian missionaries to China who taught revealed religion to the Chinese should be counterbalanced by missionaries from China who would teach Europeans the practice of natural religion.

Of Leibniz's correspondence, the most intellectually fruitful was with the Frenchman Joachim Bouvet, S.J. (1656–1730). Father Bouvet was one of the most brilliant missionaries of the late seventeenth and early eighteenth centuries. He first arrived in China in 1687, as part of the group of French Jesuits who had been equipped by the French Academy of Sciences with scientific instruments to be used in China. Sponsored by the greatest monarch in Europe, Louis XIV, Bouvet was selected by the greatest monarch in Asia, the Kangxi Emperor, to reside at the court in Beijing. In 1693, Bouvet returned to Europe at the request of the Kangxi Emperor to cultivate ties with Louis XIV and to recruit more Jesuits, whose mathematical and scientific skills were valued at the Chinese court. While in Europe, Bouvet published an extremely favorable, even hagiographical, work on the Kangxi Emperor entitled *Portrait historique de l'Empereur de la Chine* (Paris, 1697) and dedicated the work to Louis XIV. Just before returning to China in 1697, Bouvet wrote a letter to Leibniz that initiated one of the most remarkable correspondences of that time.

Whereas Matteo Ricci and the Jesuits who followed his accommodation method and concentrated on translating the Confucian Four Books had extensive contact with Chinese literati in the provinces as well as at the capital, Bouvet's circles were far more limited to the court at Beijing, which since 1644 had been dominated by Manchus. His proximity to the Kangxi Emperor (he tutored the emperor in geometry) and the imperial support he received gave Bouvet's powerful creativity free play in developing a striking but very controversial theory about the relationship of Christianity to the Chinese classics.

Bouvet was far more interested in the older Chinese classics, the Five Classics (*Book of Changes*, *Book of Odes*, *Book of Documents*, *Record of Rites*, and *Spring and Autumn Annals*), than in the Four Books. Earlier Jesuits, including Ricci, had accepted the dominant Chinese literati viewpoint in seeing the Chinese classics as historical texts whose contents were to be interpreted literally. Ricci had argued that these texts revealed that the Chinese had developed natural religion, that is, moral truths about right and wrong that were discernible through human reason and without divine revelation. However, Bouvet's analysis convinced him that Chinese characters were hieroglyphs (picture writing) that should be interpreted figuratively. This led Bouvet to conclude that the Chinese classics should be interpreted, not literally as historical texts, but rather figuratively as allegorical texts. He interpreted the book of Genesis to mean that the Chinese were descended from a biblical people who had been dispersed to East Asia. The

Chinese had preserved in their written script (Chinese characters) the hieroglyphic language of biblical antiquity.

According to Bouvet, the Chinese chronologies were wrong in claiming Fu Xi (2952 BC) as the historical founder of China. Bouvet agreed with Chinese historians of his own day who regarded Fu Xi as a mythical figure and who began Chinese history six centuries later with the three sage rulers, Yao, Shun, and Yu. According to Bouvet, Fu Xi was not Chinese but rather the universal lawgiver of all ancient civilizations who was known in different ancient texts by different names. The ancient Egyptians and Greeks referred to him as Hermes (or Mercurius) Trismegistus; the Hellenistic culture of Alexandria called him Thoth; the Arabs called him Edris or Adris; and the Hebrews called him Enoch. This universal lawgiver gave to these ancient peoples laws, customs, religion, science, letters, language, and books. In addition, Bouvet claimed that this ancient divine wisdom had survived among ancient Egyptian priests, Chaldean magi, Pythagoreans, Socrates, Platonists, Gallic Druids, Indian Brahmans, and Chinese followers of Confucius and Laozi (i.e., early and purer, not later and corrupted, Daoists). Actually, Bouvet belonged to a tradition of Christian apologists called the Ancient Theology (*prisca theologia*) of Hermetism (after Hermes Trismegistus), which maintained that certain pagan writings foreshadowed Christ's revelation. Because of this style of interpretation of the Chinese classics, Bouvet, Foucquet, and another Jesuit, Joseph de Prémare (1666–1736), are numbered among the figurists.

Ricci, in his accommodation theory, had claimed that the ancient Chinese had developed a form of monotheism and natural religion that had since been corrupted by Buddhist and Neo-Confucian influences. The figurists were much more radical than Ricci in claiming that the most ancient Chinese classics contained in allegorical and symbolical form anticipations of New Testament teachings and Christ's revelation. Figurism was such a radical theory that even Jesuits were reluctant to accept it. The Rites Controversy would force the Jesuits to completely repudiate the theory as too radical. Ironically, recent Sinological research has echoed some of Bouvet's fundamental claims that the Chinese classical texts, at least some of the older ones, should be interpreted as figurative rather than historical.

The Jesuit accommodation embodied in the production of *Confucius Sinarum Philosophus* had focused on Confucius and the classics most closely associated with his name, namely, the Four Books. Bouvet's accommodation, by contrast, avoided dealing with Confucius and concentrated on the Five Classics, which were produced prior to the time of Confucius (ca. 551–479 BC) but were supposedly later edited by Confucius. Of the Five Classics, Bouvet concentrated on what is regarded by many as the oldest extant Chinese text, the *Book of Changes* (*Yijing*). In response to Leibniz's questions about finding a Clavis Sinica, or key to the Chinese language of the sort that Andreas Müller sought, Bouvet revealed that he too was a believer in the notion of a Primitive Language, or the writing used before the Flood. Furthermore, he believed that the characters of the *Book of Changes* could reveal this universal language.

Bouvet believed that the diagrams attributed to Fu Xi in the *Book of Changes* contained vestiges of the knowledge of the most ancient human beings. However, he claimed that Confucius and his followers had confused and obscured the original meaning. Bouvet believed that only by laying aside the Confucian commentarial tradition and examining Fu Xi's diagrams mathematically could the true meaning of the diagrams be discovered. In short, Fu Xi's diagrams revealed a mystical mathematical vision that could make rational the works of God by reducing everything to the quantitative elements of number, weight, and measure. Bouvet believed that his mystical mathematical vision, which included music, was similar to that of the ancient Greek secret society of Pythagoras (ca. 582–ca. 500 BC), which attempted to explain the world through the mysteries of mathematics and music. Leibniz's mathematics confirmed Bouvet in his thinking.

In their correspondence, Bouvet and Leibniz made one of the most remarkable discoveries in the Western encounter with China. Leibniz had developed a binary system of arithmetic, which, unlike the commonly used denary system of today that relies upon ten digits (0, 1, 2, 3, 4, 5, 6, 7, 8, and 9), generated all arithmetical calculations using only two numbers (0 and 1). If we were to compare the denary and binary systems, 0 in the denary system equals 0 in the binary system, and 1 in the denary system equals 1 in the binary system. The denary 2 equals 10 in the binary system, 3 = 11, 4 = 100, 5 = 101, 6 = 110, 7 = 111, 8 = 1000, 9 = 1001, 10 = 1010, 32 = 100000, 62 = 111110, and 63 = 111111.

When Leibniz sent an explanation of his binary system to Bouvet, Bouvet responded by sending him an arrangement of the diagrams of the *Book of Changes* that showed astounding similarities to his binary system. The diagrams of the *Book of Changes* are all reducible to two fundamental elements: a whole line (called *yang*) and a broken line (called *yin*). The *Book of Changes* contains sixty-four six-lined figures, or hexagrams. Each of the lines of a hexagram is either broken or whole. Bouvet noted that if each broken line were regarded as equivalent to 0 and if each whole line were regarded as equivalent to 1, then an arrangement of the sixty-four hexagrams corresponded perfectly to Leibniz's binary progression. As applied to the sixty-four hexagrams (six-lined figures) of the *Book of Changes*, the equivalences would be as follows:

denary system	*binary system*
0	0
1	1
2	10
3	11
4	100
5	101
6	110
7	111
8	1000
9	1001
10	1010
. . .	. . .
32	100000
. . .	. . .
62	111110
63	111111

In his letter to Leibniz written from Beijing on 4 November 1701, Bouvet enclosed a copy of the A Priori (Natural or Original) Hexagram Order (*Xiantian Zixu*) in which the sixty-four hexagrams are arranged in a rectangular and a circular order (see figure 4.3). After receiving this diagram, Leibniz inscribed in his distinctive handwriting Arabic numerals above each of the hexagrams to show their equivalents in the denary system. For example, the hexagram in the upper left of the rectangular arrangement consists of six broken lines, which in the binary system would represent 000000, or simply 0. The hexagram to its immediate right represents one whole line on top and five broken lines below, which in the binary system would represent 000001, or 1. The next hexagram on the immediate right consists of one broken line on top, one whole line immediately below, and four broken lines below that, which in the binary system would represent 000010, or in the denary system 2. Finally, moving to the last hexagram in the lower right of the rectangular arrangement, one finds six whole lines, which in the binary system would represent 111111, or in the denary system 63.

Leibniz took certain liberties with the system, such as counting the lines from the top to bottom rather than the traditional Chinese manner of counting from bottom to top. In addition, this is only one of several forms

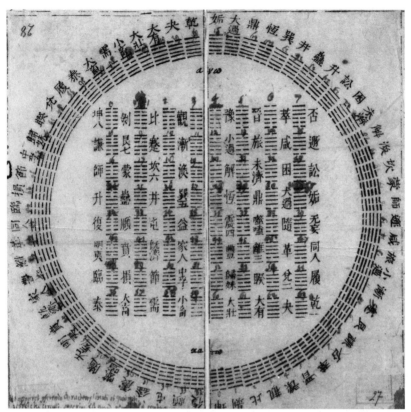

Figure 4.3.   The A Priori (Natural) Hexagram Order (*Xiantian Zixu*) containing the sixty-four hexagrams of the *Book of Changes* (*Yijing*), sent by the Jesuit Father Joachim Bouvet to Leibniz in 1701. Courtesy of the Leibniz Archiv, Niedersächsische Landesbibliothek, Hannover. The (denary) numerical equivalents have been inscribed by Leibniz's own hand at the top of each hexagram.

in which the hexagrams are arranged; in the other arrangements, the hexagrams would not reflect such a perfect binary progression. Nevertheless, these points do not invalidate the remarkable similarities. Bouvet was impressed by the fact that Leibniz's "numerical calculus" reduced counting and creation to a common mathematical basis. Bouvet believed that Leibniz had rediscovered a system that had been discovered by the Chinese in antiquity. That the greatest mind in Europe of his day had reproduced the system of the Chinese ancients confirmed their a priori nature and his figuristic interpretation of the Chinese classics. Leibniz, for his part, believed that this diagram from ancient China confirmed his notion of Real Characters and his mathematical vision by which he saw part of the principle by which

God had created the universe. We live in an age that has gone so far in relativizing truth into a function of a given culture (one culture's truths being as valid as any other) that we have difficulty grasping the visions of Leibniz and Bouvet, who saw truth as universal and absolute.

THE EUROPEAN VIEW OF THE LITERATI TRADITION: CONFUCIANISM VERSUS NEO-CONFUCIANISM

The transfer of ideas from China to Europe is one of the most fascinating but difficult trails for historians to follow. It also reveals how the Jesuits selected certain ideas of Chinese culture for transfer while rejecting others. To advance their program of accommodation between Christianity and Chinese culture, the Jesuits not only deemphasized and criticized Buddhism and Daoism but also were selective in their use of Confucianism. They promoted the aspects of Confucianism that were most complementary to Christianity while criticizing those aspects that they deemed incompatible.

Confucianism began as a teaching that revered Chinese antiquity and sages. The wisdom of these sages was transmitted in the classics, edited by Confucius. As the years passed, the Confucian teaching expanded to include a reverence for the family and ancestors, an imperial ideology, a cosmology that linked the cosmos with human affairs, an examination system by which officials were chosen on the basis of merit rather than birth, and a tradition of moral and spiritual cultivation. The famous illustration of Confucius presented by the Jesuits to Europeans in 1687 (see figure 1.1) depicted Confucius as a scholar-sage in a library rather than as a god or prophet in a temple. This depiction shows how the Jesuits emphasized the rational side of Confucianism that became prevalent in Europe.

It is important to note that the term "Confucianism" has no equivalent in China. The term was invented by the Jesuits and reflected a distinctly Jesuit interpretation of this important school of Chinese philosophy. It is a Latinization of the Chinese name by which Kong-fu-zi (Master Kong) became Confucius, first presented to Europeans in 1687 in the influential work *Confucius Sinarum Philosophus*. (The name of only one other Chinese philosopher was widely Latinized by the Jesuits in this way, namely, Mengzi [ca. 372–289 BC] who became Mencius.) The Chinese referred to this school as the Literati Teaching (*Ru Jiao*) because they claimed that the school began long before Confucius. Confucius himself acknowledged this in saying that he was a transmitter and not a creator (*Analects* 7:1). Confucius was not merely being modest here; he was absolutely sincere in his belief that he was simply transmitting the Truth (*Dao*) of the ancients. Of course, this Truth was a developing philosophy that Confucius shaped through editing the classical texts. And yet, because he did not compose the classics from scratch, it is misleading to name this school of philosophy after Confucius. The Jesuits named the school after him, not because of a misunderstanding, but because they were trying to give a certain emphasis to parts of the Literati Teaching that were contained in the Four Books.

The history of this Literati Teaching (Confucianism) might be divided into two major phases (early and later) separated by a long intervening period around AD 220–960, which roughly paralleled the early Middle Ages in Europe. During this intermediary seven-hundred-year period, Confucianism went into steep decline while Buddhism and Daoism flourished. When Confucianism revived in the tenth century, cosmological and metaphysical dimensions were absorbed through the influence of Buddhism and Daoism. The Jesuits were not the only Western interpreters of China who have used new terminology to explain Chinese culture. Whereas most Chinese scholars emphasized the continuity of the Literati tradition, Western scholars have emphasized its discontinuity. This is reflected in Western scholars' use of the terms "classical Confucianism" and "Neo-Confucianism" (which have no equivalents in Chinese) to distinguish between the early and later phases.

Ricci was the most influential voice in shaping the early Jesuit approach in China. Ricci and his followers argued that the Confucianism prior to AD 220 had been a truer form of philosophy than the revived Confucianism after 960. The Jesuits, in *Confucius Sinarum Philosophus*, referred to these later Confucians as "Modern Interpreters" (*Neoterici Interpretes*); by 1777 the term had evolved into "Neo-Confucians" (*les néo-confucéens*). According to the Jesuits, these Neo-Confucians had been corrupted by the influence of Buddhism from India. Chinese philosophers were aware that the later form of Confucianism had additional elements not found in the earlier form, but they did not see the degree of discontinuity that the Jesuits saw. The Chinese tended to see these additions as part of a tradition of continuous accretions to the same essential form of Confucianism. In their view, these accretions developed rather than distorted the philosophy, although there was debate among Chinese scholars about the undesirability of certain accretions that carried the tradition off in directions not intended by the ancients. Most of the missionaries viewed Neo-Confucian cosmology and metaphysics as philosophically materialistic and atheistic, and so they preferred to emphasize the Confucianism of the earlier period, which lacked many of these materialistic and atheistic elements.

Not all Europeans agreed with this negative assessment of Neo-Confucianism. Leibniz, for example, was fascinated by the Neo-Confucian philosophy, and some believe he was even influenced by it. The late English historian of science Joseph Needham, in the second volume of his *Science and Civilisation in China* (1956), claimed that the philosophy of organism entered into European history from China by way of Leibniz. One of the most distinctive aspects of Leibnizian philosophy is its theory of the monads. According to this theory, all elements of the world are reducible to units called "monads." These monads act, not because of any causal interaction with other elements, but because of some internal programming that has been coordinated by the creator God to guarantee that the monads interact with one another in harmony. God's advance programming of the monads to ensure their harmonious interaction is called the "preestablished harmony," and Needham believed that Leibniz was influenced in the development of this theory by the Neo-Confucian philosophy of Zhu Xi (1130–1200).

The unfolding of the Leibnizian monads not by reacting with one another but rather by a cosmic resonance is remarkably similar to the organic worldview of Neo-Confucianism. The philosophy of organism was based upon correlative thinking, which assumes that there is a fundamental correspondence between the cosmic patterns of the natural world and patterns of the human world and moral sphere. This preestablished correspondence guarantees a natural harmony. While the chronological development of Leibniz's philosophy seems to contradict the claim that he received the idea of monads from his study of Chinese Neo-Confucianism, it is clear that he did at least receive important confirmation for his theories from China and that this confirmation may have contributed to his further development of the philosophy of organism.

INFLUENCE OF CHINESE ART
UPON EUROPEAN ARTISTS

Just as European art influenced Chinese artists in indirect ways and served as a stimulus for some of the most creative Chinese painters, so too did Chinese art stimulate the creativity of European artists. However, whereas in China the influence was not openly acknowledged, and indeed appears to have been expressed unconsciously, in Europe the influence was widely acknowledged. A fashionable craving for things Chinese was led by the "apes [imitators] of China" (*magots de la Chine*). This craving produced an imaginative hybrid art form referred to by the French word *chinoiserie* that blended Chinese and European elements. It combined Chinese subject motifs with European rococo (pronounced ro-*ko*-ko) style and was especially appropriate for highly decorated textiles and porcelains. While chinoiserie appeared distinctly Chinese to European eyes, Chinese viewers would have had difficulty recognizing this art as their own.

The greatest Chinese influence was felt in European porcelains. Chinese ceramics were so technically and aesthetically superior that traditional European stoneware lost its appeal. Chinese porcelain began to be exported to Europe in the seventeenth century on a vast scale. By the eighteenth century the two-hundred-ship fleet of the Dutch East India Company was carrying tens of millions of pieces of Chinese porcelain to Europe. Chinese artisans produced export porcelain based on designs modeled on what they believed to be European aesthetic taste, and the hybrid forms were striking. Meanwhile, Europeans began to develop European porcelain centers on Chinese models, including the high-temperature kilns established at Meissen, Saxony, in 1709. The result was that porcelain production saw the greatest degree of interaction between Chinese and Europeans of any art form.

Sino-Western interchange with other art forms was more subtle. The first European to produce engravings based on Chinese models was Johann Neuhof. Neuhof had accompanied a Dutch embassy to Beijing in 1656, and after returning to Europe, he produced a book in Amsterdam in 1665 with 150 illustrations, *An Embassy from the East India Company of the United Provinces to the Emperor of China*. The demand for Neuhof's book was so great that the French text was translated into Dutch, German, English, and Latin and was widely distributed. A second book that had a tremendous influence on shaping the European image of China was *China Illustrata* (Amsterdam, 1667), by Athanasius Kircher, S.J., who was one of the most famous scholars of seventeenth-century Europe. Although Kircher had not personally visited China, he edited the reports of fellow Jesuits who had lived there. Of the many engravings in *China Illustrata*, several are based on Chinese paintings and woodcuts brought from Beijing by Father Johann Grueber. According to the art historian Michael Sullivan, one illustration of a palace woman holding a bird and inscribed by the character *tiao* (framed above her head and meaning beautiful and refined, in the sense of a secluded woman) contains the first representation of a Chinese landscape painting in European art. This illustration is a rare example among Western prints where a Chinese painting played a significant role.

The most notable example of Sino-Western collaboration on the production of a set of engravings dates from the Qianlong Emperor's wish to commemorate Manchu victories over the Dzungars and Kashgarites in the

1750s. These victories led to the absorption of the northwestern border region of Xinjiang into the Chinese empire. The emperor commissioned four Jesuit artists (G. Castiglione, J. D. Attiret, Jean-Damascene Salusti, and I. Sichelbarth) who were in residence at the court in Beijing to prepare sixteen drawings of battle scenes. These drawings were prepared around 1765 and were sent to Paris, where copper etchings were prepared at the Qianlong Emperor's expense by the French engraver J. Ph. Le Bas (1707–1783) and others from 1767 through 1774. The sixteen engraved plates arrived in Beijing over the years 1769–1775. Before the plates were returned to China, Louis XIV and some court aristocrats and Sinophiles obtained copies of the engravings. From these copies, a student of Le Bas named Isadore Stanislas Helman in 1785 produced a condensed album of engravings of the battle scenes for a curious French public.

In contrast with porcelain, very few examples of Chinese paintings found their way to Europe. Those that did had been produced by professional artists rather than the literati gentlemen artists who at the time were producing the best paintings in China. In fact, most of the examples of Chinese painting that circulated in Europe were painted on porcelain as decoration; consequently, its quality was not likely to impress European painters. The paintings that were brought to Rome did not circulate widely outside of Italy. Most of the examples of Chinese painting came through Dutch and French trading companies. The French East India Company was founded in 1660, and by 1700 substantial numbers of Chinese painted folding screens were circulating in France, along with hand-printed wallpaper and paintings on paper. This Chinese artwork was prized for its exotic qualities, but as examples of Chinese painting, they were unremarkable.

At the end of the seventeenth century, Louis XIV and the Kangxi Emperor exchanged gifts that included illustrated books from China. Using the examples of Chinese art in circulation in France, well-known artists of the age such as Antoine Watteau (1684–1721), François Boucher (1703–1770)—the favorite painter of Louis XV's mistress, Madame de Pompadour—and Jean-Honoré Fragonard (1732–1806) specialized in rococo painting. Watteau, who may have owned Chinese paintings, painted pictures that attempted to reproduce the Chinese style. Although they were accepted by his European audience as being faithful to the Chinese style, in retrospect we see that the differences were great enough to justify referring to them as examples of the completely new and hybrid Sino-Western style, chinoiserie. During the eighteenth century, there was a rage for birds and flowers painted in this pseudo-Chinese style.

During the eighteenth century, the enthusiasm for China and its culture (Sinomania) caused certain elements of Chinese culture to be absorbed into Europe. One was the ritual plowing of the earth performed by the Chinese emperor every spring. Voltaire himself praised the rite, and monarchs imitated it, including Louis XV in 1756. An engraving done around 1770 depicts the future Louis XVI performing the ritual plowing, and an etching records the ceremonial plowing that Emperor Joseph II of Austria performed in 1769. There was very little contact between European painters who worked in the Chinese court and those who worked in Europe. One missionary painter who did return to Europe was the Neapolitan Matteo Ripa (see chapter 5).

The appearance of Chinese art in Europe caused a fundamental change in aesthetic tastes. One may debate how accurately Europeans of this time understood Chinese art—clearly chinoiserie was not the same as Chinese art—but the change in European aesthetic tastes was real. The classical style, which had emphasized that beauty was the result of regularity, uniformity, simplicity, and balance (i.e., that beauty was geometrical), gave way to new aesthetic standards that prized irregularity, asymmetry, variety, and delightful complexity. Although the cultural causes of such a change are complex and difficult to define fully, it is clear that the admiration for Chinese gardens played an important role.

This movement had particular application in England, where it became part of the emergence of a broad cultural movement known as romanticism. The English garden took on many of the characteristics attributed to Chinese gardens. One of the leading proponents of this movement was Sir William Temple, who in an essay *Upon Heroick Virtue* (1683) spoke of the irregular nature of beauty in Chinese gardens. To make his point, Temple used the word *sharawadgi* (meaning picturesque), which he attributed to the Chinese but which was in fact an invented word of pure chinoiserie, that is, a European word created under the inspiration of China. Later Joseph Addison, writing in *Spectator* (no. 414, 25 June 1712) elaborated and further developed Temple's ideas by saying that the landscape of Chinese gardens tended to resemble natural landscape and was free of the artificial geometrical qualities found in seventeenth-century French gardens. Rather, Chinese gardens were ungeometrical, irregular, varied (rather than simple), and without a clearly intelligible plan.

The enthusiasm for Chinese gardens continued until 1772, when the Sinophile Sir William Chambers attempted to correct some of the excesses of chinoiserie in his *Dissertation on Oriental Gardening*. Chambers argued that the aim of Chinese gardens was not to imitate nature or anything else but rather to express and evoke passions and powerful sensations. Clearly, Chambers was anticipating the movement of romanticism here. To this end, he introduced some highly artificial (i.e., unnatural) elements in improving the Kew Gardens, the most famous of which was a ten-tiered Chinese pagoda, which was widely imitated throughout Europe. He also introduced at Kew a pavilion decorated with panels depicting the life of Confucius. However, by detaching the aim of the Chinese garden from an attempt to re-create nature, Chambers made the style more vulnerable to the shifting tides of cultural fashion. Because of the superficiality on which the enthusiasm for chinoiserie was founded, it is not surprising that it was short-lived not only in England but also in France, where both chinoiserie and the rococo style were overwhelmed by the French Revolution of 1789 and its return to classicism.

WORKS CONSULTED

Appleton, William. *A Cycle of Cathay: The Chinese Vogue in England during the Seventeenth and Eighteenth Centuries*. New York: Columbia University Press, 1951.

Barzin, Germain. *Baroque and Rococo*. Translated by Jonathan Griffin. London: Thames & Hudson, 1964.

Bodde, Derk. "Myths of Ancient China." In *Myths of the Ancient World*, edited by Samuel Noah Kramer, 367–408. Garden City, N.Y.: Doubleday, 1961.

Boxer, C. R. "Notes on Chinese Abroad in the Late Ming and Early Manchu Periods Compiled from Contemporary European Sources (1500–1750)." *T'ien Hsia Monthly* 9 (1939): 447–68.

Ching, Julia, and Willard G. Oxtoby. *Moral Enlightenment: Leibniz and Wolff on China*. Nettetal, Germany: Steyler Verlag, 1992.

Clerc, Nicolas-Gabriel. *Yu le Grand et Confucius, histoire chinoise*. Soissons, France: Ponce Courtois, 1769.

Collani, Claudia. *P. Joachim Bouvet S.J., sein Leben und sein Werk*. Nettetal, Germany: Steyler Verlag, 1985.

———, ed. *Vorschlag einer wissenschaftlichen Akademie für China: Briefe des Chinamissionars Joachim Bouvet S.J. an Gottfried Wilhelm Leibniz und an Jean-Paul Bignon [aus dem Jahre 1704]*. Stuttgart, Germany: Franz Steiner, 1989.

Couplet, Philip, et al. *Confucius Sinarum Philosophus*. Paris: Daniel Horthemels, 1687.

Cousin, Louis. *La morale de Confucius, philosophe de la Chine*. Amsterdam: Savouret, 1688.

Cummins, J. S. *A Question of Rites: Friar Domingo Navarrete and the Jesuits in China*. Aldershot, England: Scholar Press, 1993.

Dawson, Raymond. *The Chinese Chameleon: An Analysis of European Conceptions of Chinese Civilization.* London: Oxford University Press, 1967.

Foley, Frederick J. *The Great Formosan Impostor.* Taipei, Taiwan: Mei Ya, 1968.

Foss, Theodore Nicholas. "The European Sojourn of Philippe Couplet and Michael Shen Fuzong, 1683–1692." In *Philippe Couplet, S.J. (1623–1693): The Man Who Brought China to Europe,* edited by Jerome Heyndrickx, 121–42. Nettetal, Germany: Steyler Verlag, 1990.

Hao, Zhenhua. "The Historical Circumstances and Significance of Castiglione's War Paintings of the Qianlong Emperor's Campaign against the Dzungars in the Northwestern Border Region" (in Chinese). *Sino-Western Cultural Relations Journal* 13 (1991): 18–32.

Jensen, Lionel. *Manufacturing Confucianism: Chinese Traditions and Universal Civilization.* Durham, N.C.: Duke University Press, 1997.

Kircher, Athanasius. *China Illustrata.* Translated by Charles D. Van Tuyl from the 1677 original Latin edition. Muskogee, Okla.: Indian University Press, 1987.

Lach, Donald F. *Asia in the Making of Europe.* Vol. 2, *A Century of Wonder,* bks. 2 and 3. Chicago: University of Chicago Press, 1977. In collaboration with Edwin J. Van Kley, vol. 3, *A Century of Advance,* bk. 4, *East Asia,* 1993.

———. *Preface to Leibniz' Novissima Sinica.* Honolulu: University of Hawaii Press, 1957.

Ledderose, Lothar. "Chinese Influence on European Art, Sixteenth to Eighteenth Centuries." In *China and Europe: Images and Influences in Sixteenth to Eighteenth Centuries,* edited by Thomas H. C. Lee, 221–49. Hong Kong: Chinese University Press, 1991.

Leibniz, Gottfried Wilhelm. *Writings on China.* Translated by Daniel J. Cook and Henry Rosemont Jr. Chicago: Open Court, 1994.

Loehr, George. "Peking—Jesuit Missionary—Artist Drawings Sent to Paris in the Eighteenth Century." *Gazette des Beaux-Arts* 60 (October 1962): 419–28.

Lovejoy, Arthur O. "The Chinese Origin of Romanticism." In *Essays in the History of Ideas,* edited by Arthur O. Lovejoy, 99–135. Baltimore: Johns Hopkins University Press, 1948.

Lundbæk, Knud. "The Establishment of European Sinology, 1801–1815." In *Cultural Encounters: Japan, China, and the West,* edited by S. Clausen et al., 15–54. Aarhus, Denmark: Aarhus University Press, 1995.

———. *Joseph de Prémare (1666–1736), S.J., Chinese Philology and Figurism.* Aarhus, Denmark: Aarhus University Press, 1991.

———. "Notes sur l'image du Neó-Confucianisme dans la littérature europeénne du dix-septième à la fin du dix-neuvième siècle." In *Actes du troisième Colloque international de sinology. Chantilly 1980,* 131–76. Paris: Belles Lettres, 1983.

Maverick, L. A. "Chinese Influences upon the Physiocrats." *Economic History* 3 (1938): 54–67.

Minamiki, George. *The Chinese Rites Controversy from Its Beginnings to Modern Times.* Chicago: Loyola University Press, 1985.

Mungello, D. E. *Curious Land: Jesuit Accommodation and the Origins of Sinology.* Stuttgart, Germany: Franz Steiner, 1985.

———. "European Philosophical Responses to Non-European Culture: China." In *The Cambridge History of Seventeenth-Century Philosophy*, edited by Daniel Garber and Michael Ayers, 87–100. Cambridge: Cambridge University Press, 1998.

———. *Leibniz and Confucianism: The Search for Accord.* Honolulu: University of Hawaii Press, 1977.

Needham, Joseph. *Science and Civilisation in China.* Vol. 2, *History of Scientific Thought.* Cambridge: Cambridge University Press, 1956.

Rowbotham, Arnold H. "The Impact of Confucianism on Seventeenth-Century Europe." *Far Eastern Quarterly* 4 (1944): 224–42.

Rule, Paul A. *K'ung-tzu or Confucius? The Jesuit Interpretation of Confucianism.* Sydney: Allen & Unwin, 1986.

Spence, Jonathan. *The Question of Hu.* New York: Random House, 1989.

Standaert, Nicolas. "The Jesuits Did NOT Manufacture Confucianism." *East Asian Science, Technology, and Medicine* 16 (1999): 115–32.

Sullivan, Michael. *The Meeting of Eastern and Western Art from the Sixteenth Century to the Present Day.* New York: New York Graphic Society, 1973.

Van Kley, Edwin J. "Europe's 'Discovery' of China and the Writing of World History." *American Historical Review* 76 (April 1971): 358–85.

Wills, John E., Jr. *Pepper, Guns, and Parleys: The Dutch East India Company at China, 1662–1681.* Cambridge, Mass.: Harvard University Press, 1974.

Witek, John W. *Controversial Ideas in China and Europe: A Biography of Jean-François Foucquet, S.J. (1665–1741).* Rome: Institutum Historicum Societatis Iesu, 1982.

Wittkower, Rudolf. "English Neo-Palladianism, the Landscape Garden, China, and the Enlightenment." *L'Arte* (Milan) 6 (June 1969): 18–35.

5

EUROPEAN REJECTION
OF CHINESE CULTURE
AND CONFUCIANISM

The European rejection of Chinese culture and Confucianism was a broad change in attitude that gradually gained momentum throughout the eighteenth century. Unlike Jesuit missionaries who had praised China, the missionary Matteo Ripa felt compelled to leave China and return to Europe in order to advance the cause of Chinese Christianity. He established a seminary in Naples to prepare Chinese to return to China as missionaries. European rejection of China was also expressed in the inevitable evolution of the philosophes' superficial admiration of China (Sinophilia) into disenchantment (Sinophobia). European praise of China gave way to disparaging racial attitudes and the perception of Chinese people as "yellow." Christian missionaries condemned Chinese culture for allowing female infanticide, although many Chinese Buddhists and Confucians attempted to combat the practice. The visual symbolism of Europe's rejection of China culminated in the Macartney embassy's disparaging assessment of China in 1792–1794.

FATHER RIPA'S BOYS

Prior to 1800, Father Matteo Ripa was responsible for bringing more Chinese to Europe than anyone else. When he and two other Propaganda missionaries arrived at the Beijing court in February 1711, they were the first non-Jesuit missionaries to serve there. However, during his thirteen years at the court, Ripa developed an enormous dislike for the Jesuits. He was a restless man, driven by powerful motivations. After becoming disillusioned by events at the Chinese court and by Jesuit dominance there, he turned his attention in another direction, from the fine arts to the development of a native Chinese clergy. To this end, he gathered a number of Chinese boys whom he began to train. He spent so much time with these boys, who accompanied him everywhere in his carriage, that the Jesuits began to circulate criticism and sexual innuendos.

There was a fundamental difference between how the Chinese and Europeans viewed the priestly sex scandals of the years 1500–1800. While the Catholic Church regarded all violations of priestly celibacy as serious offenses, it reserved special condemnation for same-sex male relationships. By contrast, the Chinese felt that priestly seductions of Chinese women were far more serious. There was an extreme sensitivity in Chinese society over the sexual violations of women, and this was reflected in the strict separation of the sexes in worship.

The Chinese and European attitudes toward same-sex love were quite different. Matteo Ricci's perception of widespread sodomy in China was probably shaped by his exposure to sophisticated urban life among literati in Nanjing and Beijing, where same-sex activity was concentrated. The harshness of Ricci's criticism of sodomy among Chinese males needs to be viewed in light of the Counter-Reformation's active campaigns against homosexuality that had been conducted by the Roman Inquisition under Pope Paul IV (r. 1555–1559) during Ricci's childhood. While it is difficult to conceive of Ricci advocating the harsh punishment inflicted by the Spaniards in Manila in the 1580s, his comments reveal a homophobia shared by many Europeans at the time of the Counter-Reformation. And yet homosexual acts like sodomy had been widespread in Italian cities such as Florence, Venice, Rome, and, most of all, Naples. This reflected the fact that sodomy was practiced not by a subgroup of "homosexuals" (the term was not coined until around 1868), for there was no gay subculture, but by many young men and boys as a phase preceding heterosexual adulthood, which commonly began with marriage around thirty years of age.

Prior to the Counter-Reformation, sodomy had been regarded as a misdemeanor typical of *giovani* (males aged eighteen to thirty-five or forty) rather than a felonious act. Apart from occasional campaigns to suppress sodomy (the Office of the Night in Florence investigated seventeen thousand men between 1432 and 1502), transgressions were usually tolerated or lightly punished. However, during the Counter-Reformation, attitudes toward homosexuality in Europe became much harsher, and Ricci's criticism of homosexual practices among Chinese males reflected this hardening of attitudes. The Jesuit hierarchy was hypersensitive about same-sex attraction and was zealous in searching for signs of it. A Jesuit secret code that was used for confidential communication in 1601 between provincials and the Jesuit father-general in Rome included an entry "friendship with boys" (*amistad de muchachos*) that implied a sexual attraction to young males.

The homophobia of the Counter-Reformation was an obsession that caused missionaries to harshly condemn homosexual practices among the Chinese. When European missionaries began arriving in China in the sixteenth century, they encountered numerous instances of sodomy. Initially, these discoveries were made in the areas of south China where the missionaries were first active. The Spanish Dominican Gaspar da Cruz noted in his *Tractado* of 1569 that the Chinese practice this "filthy abomination, which is that they are so given to the accursed sin of unnatural vice."

When the Spaniards, filled with the religious zeal and intolerance of the Reconquista, encountered sodomy in areas where they had some control, they acted with harshness. In the late sixteenth-century Philippines, they persecuted sodomites by burning them at the stake or flogging and condemning them to the galleys. Chinese immigrants to the Philippines from Fujian and Guangdong provinces had brought with them the established and widely accepted practice of taking male lovers in which the partners assumed a typical Chinese relationship based on age, with the elder partner referred to as "elder brother partner" (*qixiong*) and the younger partner as "younger brother partner" (*qidi*). The younger male's living expenses were paid by the older man, who was treated by the younger male's family as a son-in-law. These male couples frequently lived together until well after their thirties; however, the older male also paid for the marriage expenses of the younger male if he married.

In the sophisticated Ming culture of the lower Yangzi River region, boy love was fashionable. Some criticized it as un-Confucian, but others saw it as embodying the ideals of filial piety. They explained it in terms of Confucian hierarchical relationships between an older male, who was a protective daddy figure, and a younger male, who was a subservient and filial boy. Chinese boy love involved young males (ephebophilia) rather than prepubescent children (pedophilia). For many male sophisticates of the late Ming, a relationship with a boy was cultivated not only out of sexual attraction but also because it had become fashionable in elite circles. Having a boy to love was a mark of one's elite status in society, much as a trophy wife is for older, affluent males in our own society.

There was a male homosexual tradition throughout Chinese history in which anal intercourse was practiced. Active and passive roles in sodomy were determined by age, wealth, employment, and education, duplicating the dominant-inferior roles in other areas of society. This explains why Ricci criticized the Chinese institutionalization of male prostitution among boys and actors of low social standing. Chinese did not divide men into exclusive heterosexual and homosexual categories, and many married men were enthusiastic practitioners of boy love. Homoerotic relationships were common in the late Ming dynasty and were largely tolerated by an indifferent public. When in 1429 the Xuande Emperor ordered the scholar-officials to avoid female prostitutes, they turned to boys and young men who flourished in the Ming as *xiaochang* (literally, "little singers," but actually male prostitutes). In the capital, singsong boys were hired to entertain at banquets and, after their performance, to be fondled by the guests.

The Manchu conquerors of the Ming had a more mixed attitude toward male same-sex practices and beginning in 1679 included provisions against homosexual intercourse in the Qing legal code *Da Qing Luli*. However, this law against sodomy was not rigorously enforced. These laws were part of a larger Manchu effort, whose main aim was to promote chastity. So, while public attitudes toward sodomy shifted from neutrality toward disparagement in the Ming-Qing transition, there was a boom in homoerotic literature beginning in the seventeenth century. This literary boom culminated in the 1852 novel *A Mirror of Theatrical Life* (*Pinhua baojian*), by Chen Sen. This novel presents same-sex love affairs between scholar-officials and male actors in Beijing, many of whom were also male prostitutes. While the two main characters were fictitious, most of the other characters were based on real persons who could be identified from their names and habits. The work is modeled on the most famous of Chinese novels, variously called *The Story of the Stone* (*Shitouji*) or *Dream of the Red Chamber* (*Hongloumeng*), and is a mixture of romanticism and realism.

In the Ming and Qing periods so many poor young men from the south went north in search of their sexual fortunes that male same-sex attraction became known as "the southern custom" (*nanfeng*). The Beijing wineshops became filled with young male prostitutes who worked as waiters and singsong boys for the literati. Male actors increasingly dominated the theaters of Peking Opera, where the best-looking young actors were said to come from the cities of Suzhou and Hangzhou as well as the provinces of Anhui and Hubei.

The dominance of male actors solidified when the Qianlong Emperor, out of concern for maintaining high moral standards, banned women from the Peking Opera theaters. These male actors cultivated an intensely homoerotic following that blended prostitution with acting. The immorality of actors (gambling, opium smoking, and prostitution) had led to imperial edicts of 1652 and 1770 that forbade actors and their sons and grandsons to participate in the examinations, thus closing off the primary path to success in traditional China. Consequently, the social status of actors was quite low. Nevertheless, the imperial family did not outlaw actors because they had ambivalent attitudes toward them, on one hand restricting them, and on the other hand patronizing them. The Qianlong Emperor had a particular love for drama.

The repressive Counter-Reformation attitudes of the missionaries toward sexuality created serious obstacles to conversion among the upper classes in China. These obstacles were not so serious for the peasantry because of practical concerns. The cost of having more than one wife was prohibitive to most peasants. Moreover, homosexuality was less accepted among the peasantry, with their emphasis on procreation, than in the Chinese urban areas, where boy love became fashionable among affluent and sophisticated males. But the peasants' practical preference for males rather than females made the drowning of infant girls a widespread peasant practice that was in conflict with Christianity. Only occasionally in the writings of Chinese literati does one read about open condemnations of all of these practices. One such case was Li Jiugong (baptized Thomas) (d. 1681) of Fujian. He and his brother had been baptized by the famous Jesuit missionary Giulio Aleni in 1628 when they were attending the provincial exams. Perhaps because of the Manchu conquest, Li never attained official status and remained a lowly schoolteacher. Nevertheless, he was a student of the Confucian classics and an avid reader. In his posthumously published collection of essays, *A Record of Careful Meditations* (*Shensi lu*), Li echoed the missionaries in voicing condemnation on religious grounds of concubinage, male homosexuality, and the drowning of infant girls.

After the death of the Kangxi Emperor in December of 1722, Ripa decided to take his Chinese boys to Europe. He departed from Beijing in November of 1723 with his entourage of four boys and a Chinese teacher. The oldest of the four was Giovanni Gu, who was twenty-two years old. Giovanni Yin was eighteen, Philipo Huang was eleven, and Lucio Wu was ten. The first three were all from Zhili province (around Beijing), while the fourth was from the east central province of Jiangsu. At Canton they took passage on an English ship and were harassed by the crew. They survived the crew's hostility and the bad weather to arrive in London, where King George I invited all six of them to dine at the palace. Ripa presented a copy of his map of China, Japan, and Manchuria to the king, and it is preserved in the British Museum to this day. Arriving back in Naples, Ripa overcame many frustrations, including financial problems and the animosity of fellow clerics, to finally found the Chinese College (Collegio dei Cinesi) in 1732.

The four young Chinese were the first to be enrolled in the Chinese College, although they had been receiving instruction from Ripa for years (see figure 5.1). Gu and Yin were ordained in 1734, Huang and Wu in 1741. All except Wu returned to China to serve as priests in Sichuan and Zhili provinces. Yin died in 1735, soon after returning to China, but Gu lived until 1763 and was buried in Beijing. Huang died in 1776. In 1743 at sixty-one years of age, Ripa began composing a journal, which was not published until after his death. It was widely read in both the original Italian edition of 1832 and in a condensed English translation published in London in 1844. The Chinese College in Naples lasted until 1888, training 108 Chinese priests.

THE SAD STORY OF LUCIO WU

The story of what happened to the youngest member of this group, Lucio Wu, is very sad. Wu and Philipo Huang had greater difficulty adjusting to life in Europe than the older youths Giovanni Gu and Giovanni Yin. In 1731 when Ripa was traveling in search of funds to establish the Chinese College, he received frequent letters from Huang, expressing his unhappiness and wish to leave. Later, Wu and Huang convinced two younger students to accompany them to Rome and complain to Cardinal Petra, the prefect of Propaganda, about their poor treatment at the Chinese College. The cardinal scolded them and sent them back to Naples.

In September of 1736, Huang and Wu, now twenty-four and twenty-three, went through a very disturbed period in which they were thought to be possessed by Satan. Demonic possession in the clerical world was often used to explain illicit sexual relations, in this case, probably involving mutual masturbation and frottage (sexual rubbing against one another, usually while clothed), and perhaps even sodomy. For several months, Huang and Wu had engaged in sexual play in bed, undetected by the Chinese College staff. After being discovered, they planned to flee the college together, but then had a disagreement. In 1737 Huang ran away from the Chinese College and found refuge at the convent of the Camaldolite monks. After several priests interceded on his behalf, he returned to the Chinese College. He promised to mend his ways, and Ripa pardoned him with a penance of eight days of spiritual exercises. Shortly thereafter, Huang fled again. When he was brought back from the second flight, he was stripped of his college attire, dressed in rags, and locked in a room with only some spiritual books and Chinese books for reading. Huang's isolation might have intimidated Wu and deterred him from fleeing at this time.

Figure 5.1.   Father Matteo Ripa reading the Gospel to his first four Chinese pupils, Naples, oil on canvas, dated 1818, by Giovanni Scognamiglio. Permission of the Rettore dell'Università degli Studi di Napoli "l'Orientali" (Naples). Giovanni Gu and Giovanni Yin are portrayed in the upper right while Philipo Huang and Lucio Wu are portrayed in the lower left. Ripa brought these four Chinese (aged 10–22) back to Europe in 1723–1724 and founded a seminary for Chinese in Naples in 1732 where all four youths were ordained. Through the window the Bourbon royal palace on the top of the hill Capodimonte is visible.

In spite of these difficulties, Wu and Huang made additional vows in 1739 and were ordained as priests in 1741. In the spring of 1744, in response to a request from Propaganda that a student of the Chinese College and a Congregant of the Holy Family be chosen to go to China, Ripa chose Wu and Domenico La Magna. However, something went seriously wrong because, on 25 June 1744, Ripa wrote to Propaganda asking that Wu be withdrawn as a nominee to go to China because of immaturity.

The exact cause of Ripa's change of heart is hard to discern because documents that might have explained the change are missing. Ripa listed a litany of "so many offenses, incorrigible acts" of which the young seminarian was found guilty. These included damaging the door lock to his room so that it could not be opened by his superior, making unauthorized keys to gain access to the rooms of his fellow students, and using these keys to steal nine shirts, five soutanes, six pairs of shoes, and "lustful clothes." In addition, he disgraced the Chinese College by saying that he was kept in a constant state of hunger and forced to wear disreputable clothing to prevent him from fleeing.

Code words appear in certain documents that can be interpreted to mean that Ripa decided not to send Wu back to China because he feared Wu's homosexuality might create a scandal and embarrass the Chinese College. The sexual scandals in China involving Fathers Bernardino Maria Bevilacqua and Allesio Randanini had occurred only five to six years before (see chapter 3). Like Ripa, Bevilacqua and Randanini were also Propaganda missionaries, and perhaps rumors of their scandals were circulating in Rome and had reached Ripa's ears, making him even more cautious. Like Father Giovanni Antonio Boucher, the superior who dealt with Bevilacqua and Randanini, Ripa did not see Wu's problems in purely sexual terms but rather as matters of disobedience and satanic influence that manifested themselves sexually. In the eighteenth-century Catholic Church, the accusation of homosexual activity against a fellow cleric or seminarian was rarely expressed in explicit terms. References to filthiness, madness, and demonic possession were used rather than references to specific sexual acts regardless of whether they were homosexual or heterosexual.

Wu had set his heart on returning to China and was devastated by this change on Ripa's part. On 3 July 1744, ten days after Ripa wrote to Propaganda withdrawing him as a candidate for going to China, Wu fled the Chinese College. Nothing was heard about him until the spring of 1745 when Ripa learned that he was at the monastery of Monte Cassino, one hundred kilometers north of Naples. In May he was brought back to the Chinese College in Naples.

The punishments inflicted on him by Ripa were severe. Wu later claimed that he had been unable to endure the punitive treatment and mortifications, which included eating bread and water, and sometimes a dish of dog and cat, and using whips of self-flagellation (the discipline) in the refectory. However, none of these punishments were unusual for that time. The penance of eating dog and cat remained widespread in Italian colleges, monasteries, and seminaries until at least the end of the eighteenth century. Unwilling to submit to this punishment, Wu decided to flee for a second time. Twenty days before leaving the college, he forged two documents that he planned to use in establishing his credentials as a priest.

Wu fled on 14 July 1745 and went to Rome. At the church of the Trinità de Pellegrini, Ripa's cousin, Father Giuseppe Ripa, recognized him when he was washing Wu's feet among a group of pilgrims. Wu traveled throughout the Pontifical States, using his forged documents to celebrate mass in several churches, and finally arrived in Senigallia on the Adriatic Sea. When he showed his documents to the vicar general at Senigallia, the forgery was discovered and he was arrested on 12 September 1745. The transcriptions of two interrogations (25 and 28 September) at Senigallia describe him as a thirty-six-year-old man (he was thirty-two) of short stature and squalid appearance who was almost beardless, had very black hair cut in the style of a tonsure, and wore dark clothes. Wu claimed to have resided at the Chinese College in Naples for twenty years and to have studied Latin, philosophy, and theology and been ordained a secular priest by the archbishop of Naples four or five years before.

When Ripa learned of Wu's arrest, he was struggling with not only despair but also his own failing health. He lamented in a letter to the vicar of the bishop of Senigallia that he had supported Wu with room and board for twenty-six years since taking responsibility for him on 22 April 1720 in China. Wu was sentenced at Senigallia on 29 October 1745 to a year of confinement and atonement in the Chinese College, at the discretion of the rector. Ripa ordered Giuseppe Andrada, an elderly member of the Congregation, to go to Senigallia to bring Wu back to Naples. In the midst of this affair, Ripa died on 22 November 1745 and was succeeded as rector of the Congregation of the Sacred Family by Gennaro Fatigati who shared Ripa's negative attitude toward Wu.

En route back to Naples with Andrada, Wu used the pretense of wanting to make his confession to escape. An eyewitness at Macerata described the fugitive as being short; having black hair, olive skin, a long face, and a bruised nose; wearing a black habit; and speaking a dialect part Neapolitan and part Illyrian. He was arrested by constables at Foligno on 11 January

1746. The recorded proceedings make clear that there had been a marked deterioration in Wu's clothing and appearance in the four months between his interrogations at Senigallia and Foligno. His shoes had become worn and lost their buckles, while his clothes had become filthy and threadbare. At Foligno, Wu said he was "about thirty" (he was actually almost thirty-three) and declared that his father, Tommaso Wu, was deceased. When asked if he knew or was able to guess the reason for his incarceration and interrogation, Wu replied, "I do not know, nor can I imagine the reason for which I am incarcerated." It is unclear whether this denial reflected a disingenuous lie or a state of genuine mental confusion.

Wu's case differs from that of John Hu, which has been so absorbingly treated by Jonathan Spence in *The Question of Hu* (see chapter 4). While Hu was also brought to Europe by a China missionary, the Jesuit Jean-François Foucquet, where he resided from 1722 until 1726, his situation was different from Wu's. Whereas Wu had the company of his fellow Chinese students, Hu was cut off from all Chinese and, with no knowledge of French, was unable to communicate with people in his surroundings. This produced a temporary mental derangement in Hu that led Foucquet to abandon him and commit him to a mental institution at Charenton. Wu appears to have been a far more stable personality who chose to leave his patron, Father Ripa, in order to pursue his freedom (and perhaps his sexuality).

Up until his last days, Ripa's comments about Wu had been relatively restrained, in part, to protect himself and the Chinese College from the damage that Wu was inflicting upon their reputations and to deal with Wu as an internal matter of the Chinese College. But, after Wu ran away from the college for a second time, Ripa grew hostile. He realized that Wu's misbehavior was based on a rejection of the Chinese College. Given Ripa's close identification with the college, this must have been seen as a personal betrayal as well. Ripa expressed in a letter his great bitterness toward this "perfidious Judas" whom he had taken under his wing at the age of six (in 1720) when Wu was too young to care for himself. Upset and angry, Ripa called for the most severe punishment, namely, for Wu to be sentenced to servitude as a galley slave on the pontifical ship in the harbor at Cittavecchia.

When Ripa learned that his proposed penalty had been overruled as overly harsh, he expressed in writing the wish that Wu be expelled from the Chinese College and imprisoned for life. This document was dated 29 March 1746, the day of Ripa's death, and indicates that his obsession with Wu continued into his last hour. The cardinals of Propaganda decided on 4 April to imprison Wu in Castel Sant'Angelo in Rome. Wu's fate was sealed by the unrelenting hostility of the Chinese College as conveyed by the new rector, Father Fatigati, who shared Ripa's fear that Wu might disgrace the college if allowed to return to China as a missionary. Consequently, Wu was sent from the Foligno jail to the Castel Sant'Angelo where in the roll of Easter 1746 he was listed as one of only seven prisoners.

During his first month in Castel Sant'Angelo, Wu appears to have been on his best behavior in the hope of securing an early release, but when no release was forthcoming, he had some sort of emotional breakdown. He loved to play cards but lost control of his temper when he lost. He became enraged and aggravated his opponents with curse words until they pushed and punched him. His jailers described his behavior as "scandalous" for a priest. On the occasion of the church jubilee of 1750, Wu's appeal for a pardon was rejected by Propaganda. In his appeal of 1758 to the cardinals of Propaganda for a pardon, he spoke of being a supernumerary employee in the Chinese language in the Vatican Library. On one occasion Propaganda responded favorably to his requests for assistance to pay for his care and buy clothes. But on another occasion, when he requested assistance in 1763 to treat a case of rheumatism so painful that he could not lift his arm, Propaganda declined to help. Other than that, nothing is known of his last years. He died in August of 1763.

It is unclear whether Wu learned that, in 1760, three years before he died, his schoolboy companion and fellow conspirator Philipo Huang had succeeded in returning to China. Huang served as a missionary in his native Zhili province and died in 1776. One wonders what memories Lucio might have harbored of Philipo from his jail cell in the Castel Sant'Angelo. The mind often retains memories of the distant past far better than the more recent period, especially if the more recent past has been unhappy. One wonders what he felt about his childhood companion who had shared a litter with him on that bitterly cold and windy day thirty-seven years before when they left Beijing. Did his confinement in his cell in Castel Sant'Angelo and his failing health embitter him to Philipo's success in returning to China as a missionary while he had failed? Or did he still have warm feelings for the boy who shared his sexual awakening?

How do we explain the intensity with which Ripa turned against Wu when Wu ran away from the college for a second time? Was the sense of betrayal Ripa felt intensified by his own sense of guilt for perhaps having given in to the same sexual temptations? Perhaps, but it is just as likely that Ripa since his vow at the age of eighteen had repressed his same-sex feelings in the service of God and he was frustrated with Wu for failing to show similar restraint.

The official hostility of the eighteenth-century Catholic Church to same-sex attraction was at odds with the sexual culture of Naples described by eyewitness accounts of that time. During the years when Ripa had returned from China with his Chinese pupils and was struggling to found a Chinese College in Naples, love between men in Naples was commonplace. Naples had become famous for the beauty and availability of its boys and ephebes (young men). Numerous visitors from northern Europe have left written accounts of the homoerotic subculture they encountered there.

So while Neapolitan culture tolerated many forms of same-sex attraction, eighteenth-century European Catholic priests went to great efforts to suppress any mention of same-sex desire except to condemn it. Over time Wu would probably have sensed this contradiction, particularly since the Chinese tended to be more tolerant of homosexuality. In China, same-sex attraction was usually viewed as a supplementary form of sexuality. As long as it did not interfere with the primary social duty of a filial son to reproduce and continue the ancestral line, it was usually accepted.

Moreover, Wu came from the Jiangsu-Zhejiang province region (around Hangzhou and Suzhou). This region along with Beijing and the Fujian province coast were the three regions of China where homoeroticism was most prevalent. The homosexual relationships of Jiangsu-Zhejiang and Beijing were shaped by power, status, and money. They occurred primarily between upper-class literati or merchants and lower-class catamites or male servants. Clearly, the relationship between Ripa as patron and Wu as pupil had a certain formal similarity in dominance-subservience to these Chinese homoerotic relationships.

However, it would be simplistic to view Wu's tragedy as caused primarily by a sexual conflict. It was a tragedy caused by both the spirit and the flesh. The tragedy of Wu's sad ending appears to have been caused by a deep personal disappointment over Ripa's refusal to allow him to return to China in 1744. Obedient to the wishes of his father, Wu had left his homeland as a boy and followed Father Ripa to Europe where he spent twenty-one years preparing to return to China as a missionary. While Wu's crisis was provoked by an act of fleshly desire, it became a defeat caused by spiritual rebellion. His flight from the Chinese College was an understandable reaction to an intense personal disappointment and a sense of being trapped in Europe. In the face of Ripa's resistance, there was no hope of Wu ever returning to his homeland. But the fault was not entirely Ripa's. The case of Wu's colleague, Philipo Huang, showed that it was possible for a seminarian who had committed a sexual transgression and fled from the college to later redeem himself and regain the trust of his superiors needed to return to China. In fleeing from the college for a second time, Wu spurned redemption and pursued a self-destructive path that ended with him spending the last eighteen years of his life in prison and dying there. It is, indeed, a very sad tale.

THE ENLIGHTENMENT'S IDEALIZATION OF CHINA'S MORALITY AND POLITICAL SYSTEM

Whereas the initial impetus for promoting Chinese culture in Europe had come from the missionaries, by the eighteenth century, the driving force behind this promotional effort became the anti-Christian philosophes of France. Although called by the French term for "philosophers," the philosophes were really journalists who used the new popular written media of pamphlets and books to promote their cultural agenda. Although opposed to Christian proselytizers, the philosophes proselytized with equal fervor for a different point of view. In the philosophy of Confucianism, certain philosophes found elements that corresponded closely to the ideals of the Enlightenment, and these Confucian elements were promoted enthusiastically in Europe. However, the promotion of Chinese culture in Europe gave rise to some opposition, and not all philosophes were Sinophiles (enthusiastic admirers of China and its culture). Consequently, there was a tension throughout the Enlightenment between Sinophilia and Sinophobia (dislike of China and its culture).

One great irony was that in their treatment of China, the philosophes were forced to rely upon a group whom they sought to displace as molders of intellectual opinion in Europe, the Jesuits. Both could admire the same Chinese institutions but for different reasons. For example, throughout the Ming and Qing dynasties the most important imperial ceremony of the year was performed on the winter solstice at the Altar of Heaven in Beijing. The central part of the altar, at the top of a circular structure composed of three descending levels, consisted of a shrine dedicated to *Shangdi* (Lord-on-High). On either side of the chief pavilion were tablets dedicated to the emperor's ancestors. While accommodating Jesuits interpreted this sacrifice as dedicated to the prerevelation God, the philosophes saw it as a form of rational deism.

The meaning of the deity to whom the emperors sacrificed at the Altar of Heaven continued to be an object of intense debate among Christians. In 1873 the missionary-Sinologist James Legge enraged many other missionaries by removing his shoes when he visited the Altar of Heaven because he felt he was on "holy ground." In his monumental English translation of all nine Chinese classics, Legge translated the ancient term *Shangdi* as God because he believed the ancient Chinese had recognized the Judeo-Christian God in their texts.

The philosophes had an extremely optimistic view of the power of human reason, and they believed that religion, such as Christianity, that relied on divine revelation and faith was the cause of many of the problems in society. In the eyes of the philosophes, the chaos and killing of the Reformation and Counter-Reformation could have been avoided if more emphasis had been given to human reason than to irrational religion. The philosophes sought to replace Christianity (a religion of revelation) with deism (a religion of reason). Deism teaches the immortality of the soul and the belief that God created the world but does not actively intervene in the world's running, except for an occasional fine-tuning, as in adjusting the time on a clock. In fact, the mechanical clock is a good metaphor for deism. One winds it up and it runs on its own. Since God does not actively intervene in the world, there is no reason to pray to God for intervention.

As representatives of revealed religion, the Jesuits embodied the antithesis of the deistic (or sometimes atheistic) framework that the philosophes sought to establish as the dominant intellectual mode in European society. Yet the Jesuits continued to be in the eighteenth century, as they had been in the seventeenth century, the most knowledgeable sources of information on China. The Jesuits who had traveled to China and lived there for years had acquired a deep and direct knowledge of Chinese culture and its leading philosophy, Confucianism. Practically none of the philosophes had visited China. They were like those Jesuits, Charles Le Gobien and Jean-Baptiste du Halde, who remained in Europe, editing the materials received from the China missionaries and casting it into the most favorable light for promoting Jesuit propaganda. Although du Halde was a Christian and Voltaire was a deist, both could be characterized as committed believers and talented China propagandists.

The first Enlightenment thinker to extol the Chinese was the German Christian Wolff (1679–1754). In 1721 Wolff expressed this admiration in a controversial lecture at the University of Halle, a center of Christian Pietism, which was the antithesis of Enlightenment deism. Inspired by Gottfried Wilhelm Leibniz, who had died in 1716, Wolff borrowed the idea of the "practical philosophy" of the Chinese, which Leibniz had explained in terms of ethics and politics. Wolff believed that the Chinese practical philosophy (i.e., Confucianism) contained a rational ethic that was logically consistent and also offered practical benefits to the individual and society.

Wolff and the later French philosophes shared the view that Confucianism was capable of establishing an ideal form of government; furthermore, Confucianism confirmed their belief that it was possible to have morality without Christianity. Like many of the philosophes, Wolff denied that he was an atheist and claimed to be a deist.

Because of Wolff's lecture, China became the focus of a controversy between the Enlightenment rationalists and the Christian Pietists. Wolff's Pietist colleagues criticized his presentation of Chinese philosophy on the grounds that it fostered atheism. They also criticized Wolff, a professor of mathematics, for not limiting himself to his primary field of expertise, though the polyhistor tradition—so admirably embodied in Leibniz—must have offered some justification for Wolff's delving into the realm of Chinese philosophy. The ensuing intellectual and political struggle has been oversimplified as one between religious fanatics (the Pietists) and their rationalist victim (Wolff), though recent scholarship has pointed out that the Pietists were not irrational and actually believed that learning and religion could be harmonized. Wolff's victimization was probably accentuated by the fact that he lost the political struggle when King Frederick William I expelled him from Prussia. Although Wolff had relied primarily upon Jesuit works on Confucianism, he projected his own anti-Christian beliefs into his interpretation of Chinese philosophy. Like the French philosophes who followed him, Wolff disregarded the subtleties of Chinese philosophy and religion and subsumed China's culture to the Enlightenment's cultural agenda.

Through the influence of Voltaire (the pen name of François Marie Arouet, 1694–1778) and other philosophes, China's morality and politics began to displace China's language and history as an important influence in Europe. Voltaire's primary sources of information on China were the numerous Jesuit works on China whose tone was favorable and whose contents emphasized Confucius and his philosophy. In his article on China in his *Philosophical Dictionary*, Voltaire bestowed exaggerated praise on China as a land of the highest antiquity, surpassing any in Europe. He rarely passed up a chance to criticize the Jesuits. Confucius was said to have voiced the purest morality. Voltaire defended the Chinese against the charge of atheism and idolatry. He claimed that their religion was free from superstition and from absurd legends, clearly implying that Christianity is filled with such things. Voltaire revealed his subtext when he claimed that the Chinese worshiped one God and were in communion with the sages of the world whereas Europe was divided into many groups of hostile Christians. In short, this idealized view of China is what Voltaire wanted a religiously divided post-Reformation Europe to become.

Voltaire and other Enlightenment thinkers argued that China was a model enlightened monarchy in which the emperor ruled by the rational values of Confucianism. This required that the monarch consult with the scholar-official class, a characteristic essential to the ideal of an enlightened monarch that was promoted by the Enlightenment. Voltaire believed that the cultural spirit (*esprit*) of the Chinese Confucian scholar-official elite could be an ethical and political model for Europe.

Also enthusiastic about China were the Physiocrats, whose leader was François Quesnay (1694–1774), a physician to Louis XV. In the aftermath of France's disastrous defeat by England in the Seven Years' War (1756–1763), the French sought ways of regaining their lost status. Quesnay, who became known as the "Confucius of Europe" because of his great admiration for the Chinese philosopher, expressed his proposals in a small work entitled *The Despotism of China* (*Le despotisme de la Chine*; 1767). In this work Quesnay advocated emulating the Chinese model in reorganizing the French economy around agriculture. Quesnay admired the way that Chinese scholar-officials were given power in the manner of Plato's *Republic* in which philosophers became kings. His admiration of a minimum of government intervention in the Chinese economy was the basis on which the Physiocrats originated the phrase *laissez faire* (let things alone) in an economic context. In reality, the Chinese emperors tended to intervene extensively in the work of officials.

ENLIGHTENMENT SINOPHILIA AND SINOPHOBIA

Although Leibniz and Voltaire admired many of the same things in China, the nature of their admiration was different. Leibniz's thinking was shaped by the seventeenth-century polyhistor model, which cultivated knowledge in a broad range of fields rather than primary expertise in one field. Whereas our own age would regard the knowledge of polyhistors as superficial, the polyhistor model would regard today's experts as too narrowly focused to comprehend the connections between the various parts of knowledge and unable to grasp the connections needed to attain a comprehensive view of the whole. With a scholar of average ability, the polyhistor model can easily degenerate into superficiality. However, in the case of a brilliant mind, such as Leibniz, this ability to understand the broader connections in knowledge is truly remarkable.

When Leibniz applied his polyhistor mentality to studying China, he achieved some remarkable insights. In fact, one could argue that the European understanding of China was deeper in the century preceding Leibniz's death in 1716 than in the following century. Leibniz was closer to the proto-Sinological approach, which tended to be serious and scholarly. However, the philosophes were more interested in promoting a particular intellectual program in which reason would replace religion. Many philosophes saw China as proof that reason in morality and politics worked. They praised the Chinese for selecting their officials on the basis of scholarship and extolled the Chinese system of government for fostering the development of enlightened monarchs, such as the Kangxi Emperor, whom they believed ruled in consultation with the scholar-officials. The philosophes admired the Confucian morality, which taught right and wrong without revealed religion. In fact, the philosophes practically adopted Confucius as their own sage.

Using another culture to support a cultural program is not the most objective way to understand the other culture and inevitably results in its distortion. While the philosophes' interest in China was cosmopolitan in that it drew some of its models from outside of the Judeo-Graeco-Christian tradition, it sought, not to understand China for its own sake, but rather to exploit it for the promotion of the philosophes' program. While it is unrealistic to think that any approach to studying another culture is purely objective, there are degrees of objectivity. In spite of the rather astounding misunderstandings of scholars like Müller and Mentzel and of Müller's interest in financial remuneration for his Clavis Sinica, their focus on the Chinese language gave them a degree of objectivity that was greater than that of the philosophes. Although Leibniz did not himself undertake a serious study of the Chinese language, he was very interested in a Clavis Sinica that might enable him to learn quickly to read Chinese. Among the eighteenth-century contemporaries of the philosophes in France, scholars such as Nicolas Fréret (1688–1749) and Joseph de Guignes (1721–1800) took a serious interest in the study of China and its language. Although they might be characterized as proto-Sinologists, they nevertheless subsumed their study of China to European concerns rather than studying China in its own right.

The philosophes' less objective interest in China made their interpretations of China more vulnerable to European cultural forces that had nothing to do with China. These cultural forces led to a division among the philosophes in their attitude toward China. Philosophes who saw elements of Confucianism as corresponding closely to the Enlightenment's cultural program were enthusiastic in promoting the model of China in Europe. These Enlightenment thinkers included Wolff, Voltaire, and Quesnay. They could be characterized as Sinophiles.

Other leading philosophes, such as the baron de Montesquieu (1689–1755) and Denis Diderot (1713–1784), were critical of China. Montesquieu viewed the government of China as a despotic system maintained by the threat of violence in the form of the cane. In his famous work *The Spirit of the Laws* (1748), Montesquieu defined three basic types of government: republican, monarchical, and despotic. The republican government was motivated by virtue, the monarchy was based on honor, and despotism was grounded in fear. Montesquieu took issue with the predominantly favorable Jesuit accounts of the Chinese government because he felt they had been misled by the appearance of political and social order in China. He argued that the spirit of Chinese government was dominated by fear. Montesquieu and Diderot could be characterized as Sinophobes. Throughout the Enlightenment there was a tension between Sinophilia and Sinophobia. At the beginning of the eighteenth century, Sinophilia predominated, but by the end of the century the pendulum of fashionable enthusiasm had swung decisively in the other direction, toward Sinophobia.

The degeneration of Enlightenment thinkers into Sinophiles and Sinophobes reflects the philosophes' shallow understanding of China. Sinophilia and Sinophobia belong to the categories of enthusiasms while proto-Sinology and Sinology belong to more neutral and objective categories of thought. Because the Enlightenment's understanding of China was built on shallow foundations, it was more vulnerable to the shifting tides of intellectual fashion. Sinophilia could (and did) easily give way to Sinophobia, a common phenomenon in the history of cultural encounters between China and the West. Although the Jesuit missionaries' approach was also shaped by their own program, namely, their effort to convert Chinese to Christianity, they had seriously studied the Chinese language and its culture and could consequently remain throughout the seventeenth and eighteenth centuries the most knowledgeable and leading authorities on China. The Jesuits were not displaced from this high status until the temporary dissolution of the Society of Jesus in the years 1773–1814 and the development of Sinology with the establishment of academic chairs at European universities in the early nineteenth century (beginning at Paris in 1814).

HOW THE CHINESE CHANGED
FROM WHITE TO YELLOW

Ethnocentrism (the belief in the superiority of one's culture) has been present in history since antiquity and was very much a part of Chinese history. However, theories of racial superiority are a relatively new phenomenon in world history. The division of human beings into races based on color (black, red, white, and yellow) did not emerge until the eighteenth century.

Although the notion of four human races was not developed until fairly recently, discrimination on the basis of skin color had been known since antiquity. Perhaps the earliest instance of skin-color discrimination is found in India. The ancient Hindu work the Rig-Veda (ca. 3000 BC) describes an invasion by light-skinned Aryans from the north down into the Indus River valley and their conquest of the indigenous dark-skinned people. These skin-color differences were eventually incorporated into the Hindu caste system in which lighter-skinned people were awarded higher caste status than darker-skinned people.

In the West, there is an Old Testament tradition of racial differences supported not by scripture itself but rather by Hebrew oral traditions in the Talmud. According to Genesis 9:18–27, Ham found his father Noah drunk and naked and told his brothers Shem and Japheth, who covered their father without looking at his nakedness. When Noah later discovered what had happened, he was angry with Ham and cursed Ham's son Canaan to be "a slave of slaves." Although scripture does not describe this event in racial terms, later Jewish, Islamic, and Christian scholars interpreted the blackening of the skin of Canaan's African descendants to be punishment for the sins of their ancestor Canaan and hence linked Africans with slavery.

Europeans' changing attitudes toward China over the years were reflected in their perception of Chinese skin color. These changes have been traced by the German historian Walter Demel. Europeans who admired the Chinese referred to their skin color as white, while those who regarded the Chinese with low esteem called them less white or yellow. In sixteenth- and seventeenth-century European writings, references to Chinese as white predominated, but as the eighteenth century progressed, there was an increase in the description of Chinese as nonwhite or yellow. The division by Europeans of the world's inhabitants into four or five races was the fruit not only of an increasing knowledge of the world's surface gained through exploratory voyages but also of Europeans' military and economic ascendancy over other peoples, an ascendancy that became more pronounced during the course of the seventeenth and eighteenth centuries.

Nevertheless, the idea of dividing human beings into different races was not readily accepted by European thinkers until the eighteenth century. In 1655 the French Calvinist Isaac de la Peyrère (1596–1676) published *Pre-Adamites* (*Praeadamitae*), in which he claimed that there were two separate creations in Genesis. The first chapter of Genesis speaks of the creation of a man and woman who are not named, while the second chapter refers to the creation of Adam and Eve. Peyrère interpreted this to mean that two separate races were created: humans who preceded Adam and humans who were descended from Adam. He claimed that the pre-Adamites were Gentiles and the Adamites were Jews, that is, God's chosen people. Peyrère's book was condemned by the censors, and he was imprisoned for his heretical beliefs. He was released only after issuing a public retraction of the theory. He traveled to Rome to ask for the pope's blessing and renounced his Protestantism. However, there is some evidence that he continued to hold these views in private. Peyrère's theory was very influential on eighteenth-century deists, who used it to justify their belief that the nonwhite peoples of the world (Africans, Americans, and Asians) were pre-Adamites and inferior to the descendants of Adam. The latter in the seventeenth and eighteenth centuries included Christian Caucasians as New Testament descendants of the Old Testament Hebrews.

The Italian Alessandro Valignano, S.J. (1539–1606), played a crucial role in formulating the Jesuits' mission philosophy of accommodation in East Asia, which challenged the Eurocentric understanding of Christianity. In a report of 1577 Valignano showed that he shared the Iberian lack of respect for the cultures of Africa, India, and Southeast Asia and was pessimistic about Christianity becoming inculturated in these areas. However, he was much more optimistic about the prospects for Christianity in Japan and China, whose cultures he viewed as equivalent to Europe's. Valignano referred to the Japanese and Chinese as "white people" (*gente bianca*).

The Iberian Reconquista had fostered in Spain and Portugal a concern with purity of blood that took the form of anti-Semitism, but this was not exactly the same as racism in which skin color determines dominance. Such racial theories were developed in the eighteenth century by a considerable number of the most eminent thinkers of Europe and the United States, including Thomas Jefferson. The division of mankind into four or five races began with the Frenchman François Bernier, who published his *New Division of the Earth* (*Nouvelle division de la Terre*) in 1684. In the eighteenth century, Peyrère's theory of the pre-Adamites was revived and exerted tremendous influence on Enlightenment thinkers. In 1740 the Swede Carolus Linnaeus claimed that there were four races, which he associated with skin color: Europeans were white; Americans, red; Asians, yellow; and Africans, black. Shortly thereafter, in 1749, the Frenchman George Buffon drew parallels between skin color and the level of civilization.

The Scottish philosopher David Hume published a work in 1777 that claimed that, of the four or five species of humans, only those with white skin were civilized and the nonwhite species were inferior to whites. The first to elaborate a theory of a "yellow race" was the German philosopher Immanuel Kant, who did so in works of 1775 and 1785. Kant believed that this yellow race consisted mainly of Hindu Indians who intermarried with Mongols to produce the Chinese. The philosophe Montesquieu, whose low opinion of Chinese culture was mentioned earlier, referred to the Chinese as yellow. These were only the initial theories of racial differences. The full implications of racial superiority and inferiority would develop only gradually, reaching their peak in the West during the high point of European imperialism in the late nineteenth century. At that point, the Chinese and Japanese were seen in hostile racial terms by many in the West as the "Yellow Peril." This term expressed a fear that the great numbers of the yellow race threatened the existence of the white race and Western civilization.

In the period 1800–2000, interracial marriage was viewed by many people in Europe and the United States in very negative terms. The highly pejorative term "miscegenation" came into wide usage in the late nineteenth century in the United States to refer to the interbreeding of European Americans (whites) and African Americans (blacks). Antimiscegenation laws were implemented in Southern states banning this practice and were aimed at the continued subjugation of former African slaves. These laws were finally declared unconstitutional in 1967. However, during the earlier period 1500–1800, interracial marriage was rare and regarded more in terms of exoticism; stark physical differences created an attraction that fired the sexual imagination. We have hints of a number of marriages between Europeans and non-Europeans during that time, but we know remarkably little about these unions. One notable exception was the marriage of a Chinese man named Arcadio Huang to a Parisian woman named Marie-Claude Regnier in 1713.

Huang was born in 1679 in Fujian province to Catholic converts, who, after producing four girls, had vowed to dedicate their next child to God if it were a male. Their prayers were answered, and they fulfilled their vow. Baptized as Arcadio, their son was adopted by a priest of the Society of Foreign Missions of Paris. In 1702 Huang was brought to Europe by Bishop Artus de Lionne. Rather than enter holy orders, Huang used his native knowledge of Chinese—then unique in Paris—to secure the position of assistant to the king's librarian in cataloging the Chinese books in the royal library. Huang became proficient in French and began courting Mademoiselle Regnier. In spite of Huang's precarious financial situation and warnings from several churchmen, Marie-Claude's parents approved of the marriage. For a while, they seemed to prosper as Huang became a popular figure in Parisian salons. The Huangs moved into a larger apartment and Marie-Claude gave birth to a girl. Although the baby was healthy, her mother died a few days later. Discouraged and deeply in debt, Huang died a year and a half later, on 15 October 1716. His daughter, also named Marie-Claude, died a few months later.

FEMALE INFANTICIDE

Infanticide (the killing of infants) is a worldwide form of population control that dates from antiquity. In Europe, infanticide tended to involve abandonment and exposure, while in China exposure and drowning predominated. What was unique about the practice of infanticide in China is that it was aimed overwhelmingly at girls. It was caused by poverty, by a culture that valued males over females, and by a desire for greater wealth. Female infanticide has a two-thousand-year history in China, but it ebbed and flowed, varying by time and place. It increased during periods of famine, war, and other natural disasters and was more prevalent in southern than northern provinces.

Female infanticide was by no means universally condoned in China. Buddhism was particularly vehement in condemning it. These attitudes were embodied in a Buddho-Daoist folk religion that voiced its opposition to killing girls. Buddhist teaching claimed that those who killed girls incurred bad karma that brought unhappiness and punishment. Conversely, saving little girls through personal intervention or gifts of money and food brought good karma in the form of prosperity, examination success for one's sons, descendants, and a long life. On the other hand, Buddhist reincarnation eased people's guilt by making the death of infants less final because it was widely believed that the murdered infant would be reborn.

Buddhist forces attempted to combat infanticide through the popular illustrated literature of the Qing dynasty. In yin-yang didactic style, warnings against negative examples were paired with praise for positive models. These stories illustrated the widespread belief in Buddhist karma by which karmic retribution and rewards followed in either this existence or in later reincarnations. Figure 5.2 presents a case of karmic retribution that followed a commonly believed calculus whereby the drowning of a girl would cause the death of a boy; the drowning of two girls would cause the death of two boys; and the drowning of three girls would cause one's own death. This calculus was illustrated in the case of Mrs. Zhang of Zhenjiang (in Jiangsu province). She had given birth to two sons but had drowned her three daughters because she was afraid of being overworked in raising

大劫之後報應近矣。溺死
一女必死一子。溺死兩死
必死兩子溺死三女害到
自己一命抵命。天道如此。
鎮江張氏生有兩子。恐怕
多影溺死三女後来生產。

溺女索命

女溺疹同孩兩
嬰了死時兒個

Figure 5.2. A broadsheet illustration of karmic retribution for the evil deed of drowning newborn girls. Attached to Palatre, *L'infanticide*, p. 111. Widener Library, Harvard College Library, Ch. 75.78F. The mother depicted as giving birth is surrounded by the ghosts of her three daughters that she previously drowned. The bucket beside the bed with the projecting legs indicated how the girls were drowned. A Buddho-Daoist priest stands at the right holding a rosary. Her two mortally ill sons are depicted as lying in their sickbed on the left side. The mother as well as her sons all died.

them. Later when she was giving birth to another child, the ghosts of the dead daughters surrounded her, demanding her life in return for the injustice they had suffered. Consequently, her two boys fell ill with cholera and died. Mrs. Zhang was so heartbroken that she too died, thereby fulfilling the warning.

Figure 5.3 uses an illustration and simple text to tell the story of the wealthy man Ding Zhuo of Nanchang (Jiangxi province) who is said to have lived during the Qianlong reign (1735–1796). At the age of forty-seven he was informed by a physiognomist that he would be short lived. In order to prevent this prediction from taking place, he undertook a series of charitable causes, devoting a small fortune of a thousand taels of silver to indigent people. He compiled a list of newborns and persuaded mothers not to drown their infant girls by giving each of them seven hundred copper cash (approximately seven-tenths of a tael of silver) at birth and following up with monthly contributions that included quilted clothing. His karmic

Figure 5.3. A broadsheet illustration of karmic recompense for the good deed of preserving the lives of newborn infants. Attached to Palatre, *L'infanticide*, p. 111. Widener Library, Harvard College Library, Ch. 75.78F. The wealthy man Ding Zhuo (on the left) during the Qianlong reign (1735–1796) extends his lifespan by contributing money and clothing to poor women who have recently given birth to children (on the right).

reward for doing these charitable deeds was a long life that extended over three generations of his descendants. To what extent these stories were historical versus fictional is difficult to say. However, their didactic purpose required that they be realistic and relevant to the common people's lives or else the karmic rewards and punishment would have no power to influence people's behavior.

Confucianism was more ambivalent in its attitude toward female infanticide. By valuing age over youth, Confucian filial piety diminished the value of infants. By emphasizing the family, Confucianism fostered an increase in dowries that were used to enhance a girl's prospects for a favorable marriage match. This made raising girls more expensive than boys so that families felt they could afford fewer girls. Confucian customs kept males within the family while requiring females to leave their family to merge into the families and genealogies of their husbands. Daughters were called "money-losing merchandise" (*pei jianhuo*) because the money spent on their upbringing and dowries would be lost to the family when they married. And because of the imbalance in sex ratios created by female infanticide, almost all girls did marry. Consequently, raising girls had fewer practical benefits than raising boys.

On the other hand, the primary Confucian value of treating people with Benevolence (*Ren*) led many literati to argue that killing infant girls was wrong. Moreover, killing girls upset nature's balance between the forces of yin (female) and yang (male) and created biological shortages in women. Consequently, many Confucian literati wrote essays criticizing female infanticide, and many Confucian officials attempted to prohibit it. However, imperial edicts and laws against infanticide were not strictly enforced because of the practical difficulties of policing a widely dispersed rural population and because of popular resistance to their enforcement.

In an attempt to ameliorate the plight of little girls, local Confucian landowners joined with merchants to fund foundling hospices that gave refuge to abandoned infants. Whether based on Buddho-Daoist popular religion or elitist Confucianism, these efforts to stop female infanticide were only partially successful. Moreover Chinese guilt over the practice of infanticide immediately after birth was eased by a traditional belief that life began not at conception or birth but rather upon the third day after birth, which was commemorated by a ritual "third-day bath."

Soon after arriving in China in the late sixteenth century, Christian missionaries encountered female infanticide in the form of newborn infants who were abandoned in the streets or thrown into the trash or streams. They were unaware until the nineteenth century that most female infanticides occurred immediately after birth in the privacy of homes. Usually the newborn girl was drowned by the mother or a midwife in a bucket of water kept beside the birth bed.

Matteo Ricci recorded in his journals early in the seventeenth century that female infanticide occurred in several provinces of China and that the primary cause was poverty. Catholic theology teaches that infant baptism bestows a saving grace on the child. Although the early missionaries in China lacked the material means to establish orphanages, they were able to baptize abandoned infants. Records indicate that the first abandoned children were baptized in Nanjing in 1612. However, most of these baptized infants were moribund (dying) and so did not survive. Nevertheless, Catholics took satisfaction in the fact that they had at least been saved spiritually, if not materially.

Seventeenth-century Christian missionaries taught Chinese Christians that they were obliged to save abandoned infants. If they were unable to save the infant's body, they should at least save its soul through baptizing it. Many Chinese Christians responded to this call by devoting themselves to saving abandoned infants. During the 1634 famine in Shanxi province, the number of abandoned children increased. The literati convert Duan Gun (baptized as Peter) of Jiangzhou led a group of forty literati in the Congregation of Holy Angels (*Tianshenhui*) by personally going into the street to gather abandoned children. When the condition of some of these infants was so physically repulsive that even his servants would not touch them, he personally cared for them. Duan transformed his house into a foundling hospice for one hundred abandoned children. He also assisted poor people with hungry children by giving them rice.

Christian efforts to help abandoned children were not limited to literati. Candida Xu (1607–1680) made a pioneering effort in establishing one of the first Christian foundling hospices in Songjiang in Jiangsu province. She was a granddaughter of the eminent scholar-official and convert Xu Guangqi. In many Chinese families, the baptism of a prominent family member would often lead to the conversion of an entire family. This was the case with Madame Xu. After marrying a wealthy and powerful man whom she converted to Christianity, she was widowed at the age of thirty.

She became a benefactress of the church, financing the construction of 135 chapels in the area of Shanghai, funding the publication of religious and devotional books, and generously supporting mission work and the poor. She embroidered the draperies for church altars, served as a catechist to her family, established sodalities, and supported catechists propagating the Gospel. She had a special relationship with the Jesuit missionary Philippe Couplet, S.J., who served as her confessor. She personally sewed altar linen for Couplet to take to his home church in Flanders on his return to Europe. Later, Couplet wrote a book on Xu's life that was published in French in Paris in 1688 and made her one of the first Chinese women to become well known to Europeans.

Madame Xu demonstrated a particular concern for abandoned infants. She gathered a group of women together and taught them the baptismal formula to be used on children in danger of dying when they assisted non-Christian women in childbirth. Wanting to go beyond baptizing moribund infants and procuring wet nurses for their survival, Xu sought out the assistance of her son Xu Zuanzeng (baptized Basil), who was a prominent scholar-official. He secured permission from the viceroy of Suzhou for her to buy a large house to establish a foundling hospice in Songjiang. The governor and other officials contributed, and, with her son's support, she was able to implement her plan in 1675. Many of the abandoned children gathered into this hospice were so ill that more than two hundred died each year. She purchased land for a cemetery and personally furnished the coffins and shrouds for their burials. The Songjiang hospice did not last long and appears to have closed when Madame Xu died in 1680. The efforts of Christians in China were no more effective than Buddhist and Confucian efforts to end a practice that exterminated millions of newborn Chinese girls.

THE MACARTNEY MISSION TO CHINA (1792–1794)

The year 1800 marks the end of a cycle in Sino-Western relations. Very soon after 1800 a series of humiliating military defeats and diplomatic submission would show China's glory to be a thing of the past. But even before 1800 there were signs that China's glory was ebbing. One of the clearest of these signs came through the observations of the Macartney mission to China in the years 1792–1794.

At that time the British East India Company held a state-granted monopoly among British companies on trade with China. However, because of the restrictions imposed by the Chinese government in the Cohong system based in Canton, trade with China during the years 1770–1780 had not been increased. In an attempt to improve their trading position, the East India Company had sent an embassy to China in 1787–1788, but the death of the head of the mission en route caused the embassy to abort. Nevertheless, in England the potential trade with China was viewed as so great that another embassy was planned. In 1792 George Macartney was appointed "Ambassador Extraordinary and Plenipotentiary from the King of Great Britain to the Emperor of China."

Unlike so many of the overbearing and incompetent English noblemen involved in diplomacy and the military during that time, Lord Macartney (1737–1806) was ideal in many ways. Of average height and pleasant manners, he had been regarded as one of the most accomplished and handsome young men of his day. In his active life as a public servant, he demonstrated a stable temperament, reliability, firmness in dealing with opponents, honesty, and integrity. He had scholarly tastes and was not without courage. When the French attacked Grenada in 1779, Macartney as governor was carried as a prisoner back to France. In a duel fought in 1786, he was seriously wounded. He served with distinction at the court of Catherine the Great in Russia, in the West Indies, in Ireland, and in India, where he developed a good working relationship with the directors of the British East India Company. He was also favored by the British prime minister, William Pitt. Consequently, he was an ideal choice to head an important embassy to China.

Macartney was assisted by an equally capable diplomat, Sir George L. Staunton (1737–1801). Macartney and Staunton were born in Ireland in the same year. Staunton completed his medical studies in France and attained note as a writer on medical subjects. He was a friend of the famous Dr. Johnson. He purchased an estate in Grenada in the West Indies, where in 1779 he met the newly appointed governor, Macartney. This was the beginning of a long and close friendship. When the French attacked Grenada, Staunton was also imprisoned and carried with Macartney back to France, where he negotiated Macartney's release. The bond between the two men was formed, and in 1781 when Macartney went off to India to serve as the governor of Madras, Staunton accompanied him as secretary. After he returned to England, Staunton became very close with Edmund Burke. His scholarly achievements were recognized with his election to the Royal Society in 1787. When Macartney was appointed minister plenipotentiary to head the embassy to China, Staunton was appointed not only his secretary but also provisional plenipotentiary with the authority to replace Macartney should the latter become incapacitated or die. It was intended that Staunton should eventually serve as British ambassador to China, but illness prevented him from carrying out that assignment.

The Macartney mission was meticulously planned. Since no interpreters trained in Chinese were available in England, Staunton traveled to the Chinese College founded by Father Matteo Ripa in Naples to find two Chinese students who would serve as interpreters for the embassy. He secured the services of Ke Zongxiao (baptized Paul) and Li Zibiao (baptized Jacob), both of whom had entered the Chinese College in 1773 and been ordained in 1784. Ke was thirty-three years old and Li was thirty-one. Since they had been trained to return to China as missionaries, serving in Macartney's embassy provided them with passage. They were able to translate in Chinese, Italian, and Latin but not English. Father Ke left the embassy when it landed at Macau in June 1793 and traveled overland to rejoin it in Beijing in September, while Father Li remained with the embassy throughout. Li is said to have had a brother who was a scholar-official. Upon the embassy's return from Beijing, Li remained behind in Macau, though he later sent letters written in Latin in 1801 and 1802 to Macartney. Li was praised by Macartney for his capable and honest service. He later served as a priest in his native Gansu province as well as nearby Shaanxi province and died in 1828. Ke served in Zhili and Shandong provinces, dying in 1825.

When Staunton traveled to Naples to secure the interpreters, he was accompanied by his eleven-year-old son, George Thomas (1781–1859). The young Staunton later accompanied the embassy and studied Chinese with Ke and Li. Eventually, he would exchange a few words of Chinese in the audience with the Qianlong Emperor.

In addition to the two interpreters, the eighty-four-member mission included six musicians, a machinist, infantrymen, a botanist, and the artist William Alexander, whose prints and watercolors have provided a visual record of the embassy. A collection of high-technology presents for the Chinese emperor were carefully selected. These included chemical, electrical, and mathematical instruments as well as pieces of Wedgwood pottery. The aim of the embassy was to facilitate trade by reducing or abolishing export-import duties, open ports other than Canton to trade, stimulate a Chinese interest in more British products, secure a small piece of land for use as a British trading depot and residence, and gather as much information as possible about China.

The lead ship, a sixty-four-gun man-of-war called the *Lion*, departed Spithead, England, in September of 1792 and sailed to the west across the Atlantic and then down the coast of South America and finally across the Pacific to the shores of Canton, where it arrived in June of 1793. Using the diplomatic pretext of wishing to present birthday presents to the Qianlong Emperor on his eighty-third birthday, the embassy won an invitation from the Beijing court to sail northward and land at Degu. The Chinese expended a considerable amount of money toward the transport and daily allowances of the Macartney embassy. In one sense, the Chinese saw Lord Macartney as representing a tribute envoy of higher than ordinary status. In another sense, he was viewed in traditional Chinese diplomatic terms that saw foreign ambassadors as representatives of submissive nations that came bearing tribute and requesting benefits from the emperor in return. Consequently, the Chinese placed a banner on Macartney's barge that clearly identified him as a tribute-bearing envoy from England.

There was more nuance in the diplomatic relationships of the tribute-bearing system than is often recognized. The reaction of the Chinese court to the Macartney embassy was not one of simple superiority and rigidity. The Chinese saw the embassy in terms of traditional guest ritual. The Qianlong Emperor repeatedly denied the requests of the British for more trade on the grounds that granting their petitions would invite more requests and upset the equity of the system by which foreign nations were treated in the same way. British attempts to receive special treatment from the Chinese were doomed by the obligations of guest ritual to treat all nations equally. Qianlong's court may have been perpetuating an outmoded idea, but at least they were consistent.

Although Great Britain rejected this traditional Chinese framework of diplomatic relations, Macartney's diplomatic skills made him realize that it would be unwise to make an issue over the banner. Later, however, after being conducted from Beijing to the emperor's summer residence in the cooler climate of Rehe, Macartney did refuse to perform the koutou, an elaborate bow in which tribute-bearing envoys kneeled and touched their head to the ground in obeisance to the emperor. Instead, Macartney merely went down on one knee. Nevertheless, the Qianlong Emperor observed the niceties of formal politeness. He received the letter from King George III of England, exchanged gifts with his visitors, sent his guests some food from his table, and said farewell. Realizing that his imperial audience was over, Macartney desperately tried to open negotiations with Heshen (1750–1799), the power behind the throne, but to no avail. After several days of tours, the embassy was escorted back to Beijing, and, after receiving several broad hints that it was time to leave, Macartney and his entourage reluctantly departed from the capital on 9 October.

In retrospect, the meeting of the Qianlong Emperor on that glorious, brisk morning of 14 September 1793 in Rehe foreshadowed an autumn that transcended the weather. Although the glory of China was still evident—in the majestic setting, the elaborate tent, the hordes of attendants, and the ability to control the foreign embassies—the signs of decline were present. Even the appearance of the emperor himself was deceptive. The emperor, who was about to celebrate his eighty-third birthday, was described by Macartney as looking twenty years younger. In fact, the Qianlong Emperor was growing senile. His senility had produced an infatuation with a young imperial guardsman whose handsome features reminded him of a lost concubine. This was Heshen, corrupt and corrosive, who helped hasten China of the late eighteenth century into its decline.

Some of these signs were apparent to Macartney, who compared China to an enormous drifting ship, in danger of going aground. Although the Macartney embassy was a diplomatic failure, it did obtain information that, for the British East India Company, justified the expense. This information was put to good use in Great Britain's ascendancy over China during the next two centuries until the ouster of the British from Hong Kong in 1997.

The visual art of the eighteenth century reflects the end of the great encounter between China and the West. The English painter William Alexander (1767–1816) accompanied the Macartney embassy to the Qianlong Emperor's court. However, apart from its Chinese subject matter, Alexander's drawings from this journey appear to have been untouched by his contact with China and remained distinctly European. The end of the cultural influence that characterized the great encounter is strikingly revealed by comparing two works made at similar points along the Grand Canal at Suzhou and separated by less than a half-century. One was part of a long scroll depicting the Qianlong Emperor's Southern Tour of 1751, painted in the years 1764–1770 by the Suzhou painter Xu Yang (active ca. 1750–after 1776). The other was painted by Alexander in 1796.

The Southern Inspection Tours (from Beijing to Hangzhou) undertaken by the Kangxi and Qianlong emperors were massive efforts undertaken to demonstrate Qing imperial power. When the Kangxi Emperor made his tours (1684–1707), there was still some concern about national security, but by the time of the Qianlong tours (1751–1784), the official motives were to inspect river conservation works and examine the people. However, Qianlong was conscious of his filial role as Kangxi's grandson and was eager to emulate his grandfather. Qianlong was also curious about the celebrated beauty of southern cities like Suzhou and Hangzhou. Late in his reign, the Qianlong emperor cited the Southern Tours along with ten victorious military campaigns as the two most important achievements of the first fifty years of his reign. As a reflection of their importance, both the Kangxi and Qianlong emperors appointed court artists to record the details of the tours in painted scrolls. However, while the scrolls of the Kangxi tours were collaborative projects painted by several court artists under the leadership of Wang Hui, the Qianlong scrolls appear to have been primarily the work of one artist, Xu Yang. The Qianlong Emperor's first Southern Tour left Beijing on 8 February 1751 and returned on 26 June having covered almost two thousand miles.

A major difference between the scrolls of the Kangxi and Qianlong Southern Tours is that the latter reflect a Western influence. In order to treat the scroll as a single panorama, Xu Yang employed a linear perspective that appears to have been influenced by Jesuit painters at the Qianlong court, including most notably Castiglione. Xu Yang's use of linear perspective is seen in the segment of the scroll that depicts the Longevity Bridge on the Grand Canal where the Qianlong Emperor is disembarking to enter Suzhou through the Chang Gate.

This portion of the Qianlong Southern Tour scroll, shown in figure 5.4, depicts a scene with monumental features. The length of the Grand Canal and the size of the bridge are emphasized, while the people are presented as tiny figures overwhelmed by the surrounding scene. The elevated perspective brings into view an expansive background in which the city of Suzhou fades into the countryside followed by mist and mountains in the distance. The use of mist to separate the foreground from the mountains in the background was

Figure 5.4.   The Qianlong Emperor disembarks from the canal barges to enter Suzhou through the Chang Gate, 1751. Xu Yang (Chinese, active ca. 1750–after 1776): The Emperor's Southern Inspection Tour, Scroll Six: Entering Suzhou along the Grand Canal. © The Metropolitan Museum of Art. The point of view of the imperially commissioned artist emphasizes the grand and monumental features in the Qianlong Emperor's progression. This contrasts with a painting of a nearby scene on the Grand Canal by the British artist William Alexander (below) that emphasizes the mundane and humble qualities of the scene. These strikingly different perspectives of adjacent sites in China reflect how differently Chinese and Europeans had come to view China by the late eighteenth century.

Figure 5.5.   "Barges of the Macartney Embassy Preparing to Pass under a Bridge at Suzhou on November 7, 1793," drawing dated 1796, by William Alexander. © Trustees of the British Museum.

a traditional device used in Chinese landscape paintings to convey the vastness of nature. All the activity in this segment of the scroll is focused on the emperor's movement from his boat into the city of Suzhou. This focus enhances the sense of imperial power in the viewer's eyes. This painting reveals that the Chinese viewed their land in monumental dimensions, but it is a self-image and one no longer shared by visiting Europeans.

By contrast, Alexander's drawing of the progression of the Macartney embassy under a nearby bridge on the Grand Canal at Suzhou (figure 5.5) is far less concentrated on the movement of the embassy. While the masts are being lowered on the barges to enable them to pass under the bridge, a busy but unfocused mood pervades the scene. There is nothing monumental in the Alexander drawing. The Chinese bridge is small to the point of inefficiency in delaying the progression of the barges. The Alexander drawing is almost pastoral in mood, depicting birds flying in the air and Chinese common people going about their mundane affairs. Instead of the majestic mood of the Southern Tour scroll, the view is quaint, reduced to the dimensions of a bucolic English countryside setting. It is a view of China as rustic and charming, but backward and hardly powerful or threatening. By depicting China through such a distinctly European sensibility, Alexander was conveying how little he was influenced by what he saw in China.

CONCLUSION

By 1800 the great encounter between China and the West was over. It ended because of the remarkable ascendancy of the West over the rest of the world through exploratory voyages, technology, and colonialism and because China itself had entered into a steep decline. Because of their success, Europeans and their descendants in North America thought of themselves as too far advanced to find much of substantive value in a backward nation like China. Unlike pre-1800 adulatory references to "the great and mighty kingdom of China," Westerners now spoke of the "inscrutable Orient." China became a source of merely exotic interest because of its past and was no longer important as a source of current knowledge. A few Westerners continued to admire Chinese culture and to study it seriously, such as the famous missionary-Sinologist James Legge (1815–1897) of the London Missionary Society, who made a monumental translation of all nine of the Chinese classics. However, the numbers of these Westerners and their impact were so small that they could be dismissed as students of merely curious subjects.

Whereas Chinese culture had been admired and emulated during the previous two centuries, it now became an object of ridicule and scorn. The Chinese became identified with a rigid adherence to backward tradition. Confucianism was seen as a fossilized vestige of the past. The Chinese people were looked upon as belonging to a yellow race that was inferior to whites. Even Chinese characters were looked upon as exotic antiques that were obstacles to modern learning. (In the 1950s the Chinese government came to the brink of abandoning the characters for a phonetic script.) That period of disdain for China is now at an end, and a new period is beginning. Predicting the future is a most uncertain task, and yet it seems clear that future encounters between China and the West will have far more in common with the ebb and flow of reciprocal influences of the period 1500–1800 than with the Western arrogance and Chinese humiliation of 1800–2000.

WORKS CONSULTED

Blue, Gregory. "Gobineau on China: Race Theory, the 'Yellow Peril,' and the Critique of Modernity." *Journal of World History* 10 (1999): 93–139.
Bodde, Derk. *China's Cultural Tradition: What and Whither?* New York: Holt, Rinehart and Winston, 1957.

Boxer, C. R., ed. *South China in the Sixteenth Century, Being the narratives of Galeote Pereira, Fr. Gaspar da Cruz, O.P. and Fr. Martín de Rada, O.E.S.A.* London: Hakluyt Society, 1953.

Brook, Timothy. *The Confusions of Pleasure: Commerce and Culture in Ming China.* Berkeley and Los Angeles: University of California Press, 1998.

Chan, Albert. *Chinese Books and Documents in the Jesuit Archives in Rome, a Descriptive Catalogue: Japonica-Sinica 1–4.* Armonk, N.Y.: M. E. Sharpe, 2002.

———. "Chinese-Philippine Relations in the Late Sixteenth Century to 1603." *Philippine Studies* 26 (1978): 51–82.

De Angelis, Bernardo. "Carta a los Padres Provincials de Roma a 12 de octubre 1601." *Monumenta Mexicana 7 (1599–1602)*, edited by Felix Zubillaga, 766–71. Rome: Institutum Historicum Societatis Iesu, 1981.

Demel, Walter. "Wie die Chinesen gelb wurden: Ein beitrag zur Frühgeschichte der Rassentheorien." *Historische Zeitschrift* 255 (1992): 625–66.

Dictionary of National Biography: From the Earliest Times to 1900, edited by Sir Leslie Stephen and Sir Sidney Lee. Vols. 12 and 18. London: Oxford University Press, 1937–1938.

Elisseeff, Danielle. *Moi, Arcade interprète chinois du Roi-Soleil.* Paris: Éditions Arthaud, 1985.

Girardot, Norman J. *The Victorian Translation of China: James Legge's Oriental Pilgrimage.* Berkeley and Los Angeles: University of California Press, 2003.

Gossett, Thomas F. *Race: The History of an Idea in America.* Rev. ed. New York: Oxford University Press, 1997.

Hearn, Maxwell K. "Document and Portrait: The Southern Tour Paintings of Kangxi and Qianlong." *Phoebus* 6 (1988): 91–131, 183–89.

Hevia, James L. *Cherishing Men from Afar: Qing Guest Ritual and the Macartney Embassy of 1793.* Durham, N.C.: Duke University Press, 1995.

Hinsch, Bret. *Passions of the Cut Sleeve: The Male Homosexual Tradition in China.* Berkeley and Los Angeles: University of California Press, 1990.

Legge, James, trans. *The Chinese Classics.* 5 vols. Oxford: Oxford University Press, 1893.

Legouix, Susan. *Image of China: William Alexander.* London: Jupiter Books, 1980.

Lu, Hsun. *A Brief History of Chinese Fiction.* Translated by Yang Hsien-yi and Gladys Yang. 3rd ed. Beijing: Foreign Language Press, 1976.

Macartney, George. *An Embassy to China, Being the Journal Kept by Lord Macartney during His Embassy to the Emperor Ch'ien-lung 1793–1794.* Edited by J. L. Cranmer-Byng. London: Longmans, 1962.

Mackerras, Colin P. *The Rise of the Peking Opera 1770–1870: Social Aspects of the Theatre in Manchu China.* Oxford: Clarendon, 1972.

———. *Western Images of China.* Hong Kong: Oxford University Press, 1991.

McKee, David Rice. "Isaac de la Peyrère, a Precursor of Eighteenth-Century Critical Deists." *PMLA* 49 (1944): 456–85.

Meijer, M. J. "Homosexual Offences in Ch'ing Law." *T'oung Pao* 71 (1985): 109–12.

Mungello, D. E. "Aus den Anfängen der Chinakunde in Europa, 1687–1770." In *China illustrata: Das europäische Chinaverständnis im Spiegel des sechszehnten bis achtzehnten Jahrhundert*, edited by Hartmut Walravens, 67–78. Weinheim, Germany: Acta Humaniora, 1987.

———. "Confucianism in the Enlightenment: Antagonism and Collaboration between the Jesuits and the Philosophes." In *China and Europe: Images and Influences in Sixteenth to Eighteenth Centuries*, edited by Thomas H. C. Lee, 99–127. Hong Kong: Chinese University Press, 1991.

———. *Drowning Girls in China: Female Infanticide since 1650*. Lanham, Md.: Rowman & Littlefield, 2008.

———. "The Sad Tale of Lucio Wu (1713–1763)." *Sino-Western Cultural Relations Journal* 29 (2007): 19–33.

———. *The Spirit and the Flesh in Shandong, 1650–1785*. Lanham, Md.: Rowman & Littlefield, 2001.

New Catholic Encyclopedia. Washington, D.C.: McGraw-Hill, 1967.

Ng, Vivien W. "Homosexuality and the State in Late Imperial China." In *Hidden from History: Reclaiming the Gay and Lesbian Past*, edited by Martin B. Duberman et al., 76–89. New York: New American Library, 1989.

Palatre, Gabriel, S.J. *L'infanticide et l'oeuvre de la Sainte-Enfance en Chine*. Shanghai: Mission catholique à l'orphelinat de Tou-sè-wè, 1878.

Pelliot, Paul. "Les 'Conquêtes de l'empereur de la Chine.'" *T'oung Pao* 20 (1921): 183–274.

Popkin, Richard H. "The Philosophical Basis of Eighteenth-Century Racism." In *Studies in Eighteenth-Century Culture*. Vol. 3, *Racism in the Eighteenth Century*, edited by Harold E. Pagliaro, 245–62. Cleveland: Case Western Reserve University Press, 1973. See also in the same volume "Symposium Introduction," 239–43.

Reichwein, Adolf. *China and Europe: Intellectual and Artistic Contacts in the Eighteenth Century*. Translated by J. C. Powell. London: Kegan Paul, 1925.

Ripa, Matteo. *Memoirs of Father Ripa during Thirteen Years' Residence at the Court of Peking in the Service of the Emperor of China*. London: John Murray, 1844.

———. *Storia della fondazione della Congregazione e del Collegio de'Cinesi*. 3 vols. Naples: Manfredi, 1832.

Rivinius, Karl Josef. *Das Colloquium Sinicum zu Neapel und seine Umwandlung in ein Orientalisches Institut*. Nettetal, Germany: Steyler Verlag, 2004.

Rocke, Michael. *Forbidden Friendships: Homosexuality and Male Culture in Renaissance Florence*. New York: Oxford University Press, 1996.

Ross, Andrew C. *A Vision Betrayed: The Jesuits in Japan and China, 1542–1742*. Edinburgh: Edinburgh University Press, 1994.

Spence, Jonathan D. "The Paris Years of Arcadio Huang." In *Chinese Roundabout: Essays in History and Culture*, 11–24. New York: W. W. Norton, 1992.

Vitiello, Giovanni. "The Dragon's Whim: Ming and Qing Homoerotic Tales from the Cut Sleeve." *T'oung Pao* 78 (1992): 341–72.

Wickberg, Daniel. "What Is the History of Sensibilities? On Cultural Histories, Old and New." *American Historical Review* 112 (2007): 661–84.

Wolff, Christian. *Oratio de Sinarum philosophia practica: Rede über die praktische Philosophie der Chinesen.* Translated by Michael Albrecht. Latin and German texts. Hamburg, Germany: Felix Meiner, 1985.

INDEX

assimilation, Christianity in China, 25,
28, 48. *See also* accommodation,
inculturation of Christianity
astrology, 62–63
astronomy, 21, 34–35, 62–63
atheism, 105, 126, 127
Attiret, Jean-Denis, S.J., 67, 108
Augustinians, 18

Babel, confusion of tongues, 89, 95
"Ballad of East and West" (Kipling), 12
baptism, 27, 55, 86; infants, 137; Three
Pillars, 21–22
barbarians, 5
baroque style, 40, 74, 76
Barros, João de, 81
Beijing National Library, 77
Beijing, 19, 25, 29, 140, 142; imperial
court, 34–37, 39, 99, 108, 113, 141;
urban life, 114
Beitang (North Church), 40, 66
Belleville, Charles de, S.J., 66
benefactress, 138
Benevolence *(Ren)*, 137
Berlin Staatsbibliothek, 91
Berlin. *See* Brandenburg-Berlin court
Bernier, François, 132
Bevilacqua, Bernardino Maria, O.F.M.,
58, 120
Bianji (Varo), 29
Bible: adherence to, 43; chronology, 93;
patriarchs, 54, teaching, 13
binary system, 101–104
black magic, 32, 57. *See also* magical
arts
black race, 131–133
blood, purity of, 132
Bochen school, 71
bodhisattva, 65; costume, 70. *See also*
Guanyin
Boucher, Fr. Giovanni Antonio, 59, 120
Boucher, François, 108
Bourbons, 119

Bouvet, Joachim, S.J., 40, 66, 99–108
Boxer Rebellion, 11
boys: love of young males
(ephebophilia), 115–116, 124; sexual
relations, 114
Brahmans, 100
Brandenburg-Berlin court, 90, 91
Braunschweig, house of, 89
British East India Company, 139, 142
Bu Ru wengao (Shang), 23–24
Buddha, 22
Buddhism, 5, 34, 41, 53, 64: art, 43;
corrupting influence, 100; golden
age in China, 32, 105; hell, 32;
influence on Confucianism, 9, 105;
Jesuits adopt monks' clothing, 20;
lotus, 27; Ming syncretism, 21–23;
opposed female infanticide, 113,
134; refuge of poor, 20; rejected by
Chinese literati, 23, 54; rejected in
Jesuit accommodation, 21, 86, 104;
secret societies, 27–28; self-beating
(zipu), 26; sexual immorality of
monks, 19; wandering monks, 57.
See also bodhisattva
Buddho-Daoism, 23, 48, 134, 135, 137
Budeyi (Yang), 45–46, 63
Buffon, George, 132
Buglio, Ludovici, S.J., 41
Bureau of Astronomy, 34–35, 62–63,
76; Chinese astronomers, 63. *See also*
calendar
Burke, Edmund, 140

Caballero a Santa Maria, Antonio,
O.F.M., 23, 25–26
Cahill, James, 71–74
Calabria, 58
calculator/calculus, Leibniz, 89
calendar, 63
Calvinism (Reformed Church), 17;
Dutch, 18
Calvinists, 90, 131; Dutch, 18, 37

ABOUT THE AUTHOR

D. E. Mungello, the grandson of Italian and German immigrants to the United States, first became interested in Sino-Western history as a graduate student at the University of California at Berkeley. This interest led to three years of postdoctoral research in Germany as an Alexander von Humboldt fellow and Herzog August Bibliothek Wolfenbüttel fellow. He has published numerous articles and books on Sino-Western history, several of which have appeared in Chinese and Korean editions. He is the founder and editor of the *Sino-Western Cultural Relations Journal*. His most recent book is *Drowning Girls in China: Female Infanticide since 1650*. His first teaching position was at Lingnan College in Hong Kong, and he is currently professor of history at Baylor University in Waco, Texas.